1969

Are you still listening?

STORIES AND ESSAYS

Brent Green

Carol Orsborn, Ph.D.
David Cogswell
Richard Adler
Bob Moses
Jed Diamond, Ph.D.
Greg Dobbs
Robert William Case

Brent Green & Associates, Inc.
Denver, Colorado
2019

Book Copyright © 2019 by Brent Green & Associates, Inc.
All rights reserved.
Copyrights for chapter contributions by authors other than Brent Green
remain with each contributing author.

No part of this publication may be reproduced, distributed or transmitted in any form or by any means, including photocopying, recording, or other electronic or mechanical methods, without the prior written permission of the publisher, except in the case of brief quotations embodied in critical reviews and certain other noncommercial uses permitted by copyright law. For permission requests, write to the publisher, addressed "Attention: Permissions Coordinator," at the address below.

Brent Green & Associates, Inc.
1011 S. Valentia St., Suite 86
Denver, Colorado 80247

ISBN-10: 0-578-48845-0
ISBN-13: 978-0-578-48845-5

Visit the book website: http://www.1969stories.com

Printed in the United States of America

Book cover design by Barry Merten, Merten Design Group, Denver

Book Layout ©2017 BookDesignTemplates.com

Publisher's Note: Some chapters in this book are works of fiction. Names, characters, places, and incidents are a product of the author's imagination. Locales and public names are sometimes used for atmospheric purposes. Any resemblance to actual living persons or to businesses, companies,
institutions or locales is completely coincidental.

1969: Are you still listening? / Brent Green —1st ed.

Contents

Summer of '69 in Moochville 1

Did You Know the Sun Was Shining? 9

The Black Armband 15

A Report from the Scene 25

Double-Crossed 37

The Peak of American Civilization 55

Cat's in the Cradle 63

Hell No! 75

Freedom Tastes of Reality 93

Of Miniskirts, Misdeeds, and Moon Missions 103

I Pledge Allegiance 109

The Promise 121

Flash of White 129

Guns, Wings, & Rites of Passage 139

Postscript: Reflections on Kent State 157

A Sizzling Dream of Imagination 163

Afterword: Woodstock—Toward A Better America? 167

About the Authors 173

Carol Orsborn, Ph.D. 175

David Cogswell 177

Richard Adler 179

Bob Moses 181
Jed Diamond, Ph.D. 183
Greg Dobbs 185
Robert William Case 187
Brent Green 189

Dedicated to men and women who not only remember the sixties but have contributed to constructive social, economic and political changes, from then until now.

"By and large, the past two generations have made such a colossal mess of the world that they have to step down and let us take over."
—PETE TOWNSHEND

"We've got this gift of love, but love is like a precious plant. You can't just accept it and leave it in the cupboard or just think it's going to get on by itself. You've got to keep on watering it. You've got to really look after it and nurture it."
—JOHN LENNON

"When you've seen beyond yourself, then you may find, peace of mind is waiting there."
—GEORGE HARRISON

"Power, no matter what kind of power it is, without a foundation in truth, is a dictatorship, more or less and in one way or another, for it is always based on man's fear of the social responsibility and personal burden that 'freedom' entails."
—WILHELM REICH

"Let us begin the revolution and let us begin it with love: All of us, black, white, and gold, male and female, have it, within our power to create a world we could bear out of the desert we inhabit for we hold our very fate in our hands."
—KATE MILLET

Introduction

Crosby, Stills & Nash. Their inimitable mingling of harmonies was magical as if an angelic chorus. Their songs crooned of love and love lost, of exotic travels and foreign places, and of transcendental life experiences. Before they began their half-a-century journey together, each band member had already become a folk-rock celebrity, but then they were three together and for each other.

One early spring day in 1969, they convened for a photoshoot with acclaimed rock 'n' roll photographer Henry Diltz. Their mission: an album cover that would make a statement. Nothing fancy or overly manicured. They insisted on a location that felt "downhome and comfortable" like their music.

Thus, they selected a besieged dwelling, a wood-frame house once occupied by hardscrabble railroad workers and located near Santa Monica Boulevard in West Hollywood, California. Their laid-back photo featured the musicians seated on a tattered couch in front of the dilapidated house.

The three superstars wore unpretentious attire popular for fashionable men of that year: faded blue jeans with cowboy boots (Nash and Crosby) and hiking boots (Stills). It's ironic also that a monumental musical achievement would become packaged and sold with the help of an iconic setting, downtrodden and fleeting, just as youthful generations felt empowered to become free of uptight conventions and conformity.

They had not yet selected a name for their band, so they did not pay close attention to seating order. Lack of conceptual clarity could be easily dismissed then, reflecting a mood of 1969. They dodged apprehension about things that should not matter—avoiding pretense at all costs—staying focused on issues that did matter such as social and political activism. Ending the war in Vietnam. Equal rights. Power to the people. Sex, drugs, and rock 'n' roll. The times were uncertain and stormy in the lives of these band members as well as the millions who fell in love with their music.

A few days later, after much thought and debate, they finally agreed to use their surnames to brand the band, a wise decision to prevent the band from enduring after just one of its members departed or died. With Crosby's name leading, the resolved naming order would not then match the cover photo, with Nash on the left side, Stills in the middle, and Crosby on the right.

They returned to the same location to reshoot the cover only to discover that the house had already been torn down; all that remained was a pile of lumber. Even the butt-ugly couch had vanished. Starting over was not an option.

Well, whatever. The music came first.

In May 1969, David Crosby, Stephen Stills, and Graham Nash released their finished album. The eponymously titled LP record, *Crosby, Stills & Nash*, became a runaway success in the United States and Europe.

This inaugural cocreation reached a sales crescendo at #6 on the Billboard album chart, staying on the chart for 107 weeks. The album gave birth to two Top 40 hits, including "Suite: Judy Blue Eyes" (#21) and "Marrakesh Express" (#28). Their foundational artistic triumph achieved quadruple platinum certification in 2001, exceeding over four million in U.S. sales.

One song from their hit-filled catalog rose above the rest. Stephen Stills wrote a ballad during a time when separation from his famous girlfriend, Judy Collins, was inevitable. Both were huge stars with impossible traveling and performing schedules, and they could not reconcile their careers and a long-distance relationship. During dark hours of lonely reflection, Stills penned "Suite: Judy Blue Eyes." One verse rings true, honest, and vulnerable:

Something inside is telling me that I've got your secret
Are you still listening?

The writer created an ode to past times and how he will miss them—what the couple enjoyed when they had each other. Classic rock's greatest breakup song is a summary of the unsettled past, an apology for an ambiguous present, and a glimpse into an uncertain future.

This is distilled truth, not only for famous lovers but also for a generation of fans able to identify with unrequited love and thwarted ambitions. Most young adults back then could ask the same galvanizing question of their peers, lovers, parents, elected representatives, communities, and nation: *Are you still listening?*

Now, as those who lived through that concluding year of a tumultuous decade reach their final decades in the 21st century, some continue to ask if leaders who chart the course of the nation are listening. Are younger generations listening? Are disparate races and cultures listening to each other? Is the world listening?

Some wonder: can we learn from the past about the forces that inexorably shaped our lives today? Can we ease a persistent climate of discord and suspicion? Can we rediscover softer melodies of hope and renewal? Will we learn from our mistakes?

For those who lived through a boisterous year that was 1969, are we still listening to the hopes and dreams expressed by youth from that pivotal year? Do we hear their fears as we confront today's mendacious and self-serving manipulators?

Let the past remind us of what we are not now. Because *we* are still listening.

CHAPTER ONE

Summer of '69 in Moochville

By Brent Green

I rock 'n' rolled into 1969 at age 19: young enough to be uninhibited, old enough to be reflective about lapses of inhibition. Bounded by 6 caressing 9, the final year of the sixties turned epochal, oozing innuendo and liberated promises as rigid Texas traditions collided with gritty young adults keen on relaxing too many uptight values.

Houston in 1969 lacked abundant summer jobs. The Baby Boomer age-wave had flooded the job market that summer, and even Ronald McDonald offered scant opportunities for students eager to fry hamburgers. I spent a couple of fruitless weeks scanning newspaper ads and filling out employment applications, feeling oppressed by my dad's practical expectations that I get a summer job—any job that would get me up in the morning and out of the house.

One day I discovered a newspaper ad with an alluring headline:

STUDENTS!

Win a Trip to Madrid, a New Mustang Convertible and Cash Awards! Great Career Opportunities!

The scintillating staffing ad encouraged highly motivated students to attend a kick-off rally at a downtown hotel. Slackers need not apply. Two days later several hundred scholarly opportunists packed a ballroom. I had arrived early to snag a good seat, epitomizing in my demeanor extraordinary enthusiasm. I needed this job before I understood its dimensions and strictures.

Bob Oliver and Richard Harris escorted a rapt audience through an elaborate spiel. Quaffed and expensively dressed, the middle-aged men suspended disbelief that any summer job could be so promising in such a shitty employment market. They made it all seem possible whatever it was. Younger acolytes, already part of their team, bubbled with confident gusto and shared earnest testimonials. Bundles of money would be paid. Status would come with almost effortless work. Other intangible rewards would follow: self-esteem, marketing knowhow, worldliness, and powerful people skills. And don't forget about an all-expense-paid trip to Madrid or a 1969 Mustang convertible. It took an hour before the bombastic hosts finally revealed their bottom line: they were offering commission-only jobs to peddle a recently published home library attractively named *Merit Students Encyclopedia*, published by Collier's.

Jobless and tense over escalating parental censure for being jobless, I accepted the job once I was selected, which meant that I had been willing to stick around following the presentation and proclaim my faith in materialism. "I'd love to win the Mustang—in fact, that's exactly what I intend to do!"

Dad thought it would be an enduring formative experience, although he wasn't destined to lug a briefcase door-to-door in sizzling heat and humidity while invading track-home sameness from Galveston to El Paso with the immense yawn of southwest Texas in-between.

Following a day of exhaustive training in Houston and a homework mandate to memorize a presentation script word-for-word, the summer of a lifetime unfolded into the Lone Star State's untrammeled and sometimes ignorant byways. The entire Texas sales force journeyed by day, hip-hopping towns from Houston to El Paso during a god-awful searing summer. We traveled in a caravan of four sedans and a convertible packed with positive but penurious students trying to make a few bucks and get through the summer.

Our crew featured interesting diversity. David, a Harvard divinity student, could cite poignant scriptures to defrock any argument that the Vietnam War was morally justifiable. Sarah, a towering hippie chick with waist-length hair and Twiggy legs, became proficient at selling books beyond logical explanation. And Ed, an unemployed rock 'n' roll DJ with a velvet baritone voice capable of seducing bored housewives, had been a roadie for the Southern-rock group Lynryd Skynrd when the Florida band was still known as My Backyard.

Bob and Richard targeted neighborhoods populated by ticky-tacky box houses lined up in symmetrical rows, pastel stucco or fiberboard exteriors, swing sets in backyards, Corvairs or Chevelles parked on driveways. They scouted for indicators of patriotism, naivete and ambition, the Trinity of door-to-door sales success.

Moochville, U.S.A.

They crawled middle-class neighborhoods in their luxury vehicles—displaying ostentatious arrival statements for the benefit of nosy neighbors—while selecting suburbs lacking convenience stores. We couldn't then escape into air-conditioned comfort and wile away evenings playing pinball games. At 4:00

p.m., they deposited us at strategic cross sections of uncaring, uninviting, unimaginative expanses of monotony.

Briefcases in hand, neckties knotted, chicks' make-up seductive but understated, we knocked on doors for six hours and returned to our drop-off spots promptly at 10:00. Our mission between drop-off and pick-up was to get inside as many houses as possible and sell books. A Texas blast furnace inspired us to keep knocking on doors and ringing doorbells, sometimes for six unfulfilling hours during nightmare dry spells.

Both Mom and Dad Mooch needed to be present and willing to answer qualifying questions. Our explicit purpose was to give away encyclopedia sets. Yes, free of charge for the lucky family that met requirements for such an incredible gift of learning. We weren't selling anything.

We qualified victims as to their suitability for this lofty honor, a beneficent gesture from Collier's, the educational brand they could trust. We called it "sample advertising." Their only obligation—assuming the books delivered everything we promised—would be to write an enthusiastic testimonial for use in company advertising. A sleight-of-hand arrived about the time Mooches visualized their kids trotting off to Stanford or Harvard, thus liberated from the same ticky-tacky existence as their parents' plight. The qualifying pitch made certain that parents highly valued education for their children. We asked again—several times. They declared allegiance to prescribed moral commitments before we arrived at the closing question.

Social psychologists call our powerful sales tactic the Foot-in-the-Door Technique. This involved coaxing captivated Mooches, gaining concurrence with core values such as the importance of learning, knowledge, and higher education. The more that Mooches affirmed verbal agreement with qualifying questions, the more likely they would feel obligated to go along with a final large request to fork over serious money for their very own encyclopedia library, plus a two-volume dictionary, plus a twenty-volume set of *The Harvard Classics*.

1969: Are You Still Listening?

Sales manager Richard Harris—who was unrelated to the famous actor but relished the name association, sporting black Ray Bans and radiating Hollywood swagger—taught his sales scholars to think of each confirmatory answer to a qualifying question as slamming an imaginary door. He calculated that a successful presentation would close thirteen doors, thus trapping the target Mooch, cage-like. Once the final door slammed, Mooches could not escape the situation without a serious case of cognitive dissonance. Most of those qualified would then write checks, sometimes in an altered state of consciousness.

Are you curious about the too-good-to-be-true catch?

After Mom and Dad Mooch had embraced learning and education with their enthusiastic pronouncements, it followed that they must be the kind of parents who would keep a free twenty-five-volume set up-to-date. ("Just like regular oil changes for that Chevelle parked on the driveway.") This they could accomplish by ordering annual yearbooks featuring scientific discoveries and major events from the previous year.

The update service was not free, and we asked them to pay upfront for ten consecutive years. Mr. and Mrs. Mooch, being conscientious parents, then agreed to shell out 34 cents every day to save for their annual yearbooks. We demonstrated the math for them by dropping exact change into a plastic coin bank, also included with all the wonderful books.

A profitable number of Mooch couples—Corvairs parked on driveways, swing sets in backyards—could be transitioned in about ninety minutes from disgust over an uninvited doorbell near dinnertime to elation over forthcoming Ivy League education for their munchkins. Some Mooches became virtuous when finally signing a contract for $1,200 (valued at over $8,000 today!). They handed over deposit checks for $200. When we nailed the pitch, they would bid us farewell as a new family friend, delighted to have been selected as their neighborhood's official sample advertising family.

[5]

My hands sometimes trembled when I presented signed contracts and deposit checks to Richard Harris. He was an exuberant man to please, almost worth the psychic cost of many rejections, night after night. His confident hand would reach over and pump mine vigorously. "All right, Brother Brent!" he would proclaim with a wide grin.

The average rep closed a Mooch couple every few nights—sometimes knocking on several hundred doors to land a big score. The best of us, such as hippie Sarah, could sometimes land two sales in a single night. She became legendary for one time closing three sales in six hours, and a few dudes cynically attributed her prowess to miniskirts showcasing astonishing legs. Because the commission for each set was a cool $200, that nubile, nymph-like bohemian lady took in almost two grand some weeks. That wasn't pocket change in 1969.

But financial glory included risks. The company never purchased sales licenses for 31 clueless college students, and almost every night somebody got busted. Texas enforced the Green River Ordinance with vengeance, a law prohibiting door-to-door sales without local licenses. Buying 31 licenses every night wasn't practical or affordable. Richard and Bob played the odds; we played their victims.

One time in Austin a balding, bulging Mooch threatened to beat me up after I disqualified his family. He didn't agree with the required qualifying commitments, so, as instructed, I informed him that he and the missus weren't educationally minded enough to be selected as a sample advertising family. Bad choice of phrasing.

He called the cops after I departed his living room, which led to a curbside interrogation, a one-way trip to the police station, and the indignities of a criminal booking. Then I spent two anxious hours in the Austin city jail with hardened convicts checking me out as tie-clad teenage meat. Embellished in his hand-tailored dress shirt and a five-hundred-dollar suit, luminous Richard Harris eventually arrived and bailed me out with a gleaming smile. The cavalcade rolled on to San Antonio the next morning as if nothing weird or worrisome had happened. Just another day in the book biz.

When we weren't selling, we partied into the wee hours at seedy motels. Sexual liaisons happened among the young and impetuous, including all of us. With Texas being the nation's most punitive state concerning possession or use of marijuana, we often became frustratingly "head starved," but we found creative ways to tune in and turn on, sometimes through the resourcefulness of Bud, a worldly Vietnam vet who had army buddies in many Texas towns. We also discovered the potential of over-the-counter Robitussin, a cold medication spiked with dextromethorphan. The surprising psychedelic effects served psychic purposes in addition to coughing cessation.

Being at least fifteen years older than their charges, Bob and Richard didn't know what we were doing, but they distrustfully insisted that we do it in the same motel room and not invade swimming pools or public spaces. They tolerated our budding countercultural ways because we brought them paychecks large enough to provide a steady flow of designer suits and self-conscious slip-on loafers.

Free enterprise rocketed with the roll in southern Texas throughout those blistering months defined by Neil Armstrong's first steps on the moon and a legendary rock concert in Upstate New York called Woodstock. Thirty-one hippies and antiwar activists traded psychoactive substances and romantic partners with carefree abandon, and many sold their way to amazing profitability during the summer of '69. My dad was impressed with my sales pluck and ingenuity though nervous about his boy suddenly becoming a more self-assured young man with combative opinions.

Our motley crew knocked on thousands of strangers' doors, started an experimental commune in downtown Houston to explore alternative lifestyle options under the same roof, sampled substances still pharmacologically unclear, made a substantial amount of money, and readied ourselves for cultural and social upheavals that would beset university campuses that coming fall semester.

Thanks to *Merit Students Encyclopedia* and Collier's, we were primed, pumped and prepared for forthcoming strange changes, mostly as meritorious college students wise to the ways of Mooch manipulation.

Tailpiece

I never found out who won a trip to Madrid or a new Mustang, the incentives most alluring to me in that fateful newspaper want-ad. Fictitious come-ons, I now presume. But I did win a Deluxe Edition of *The Harvard Classics*, today gracing my living room bookshelf—a satisfying symbol and reminder of my slap-dash youth. Bob Oliver, an ironic spitting image of actor Dustin Hoffman, offered me a sales territory in San Antonio instead of returning to the university. I turned him down. He vigorously shook my hand while escorting me from his office as if disqualifying a reticent Mooch.

CHAPTER TWO

Did You Know the Sun Was Shining?

By Carol Orsborn, Ph.D.

At 70, I am reaping a level of psychological and spiritual freedom rooted fifty years ago in the rich soil of 1969. I can say this, even while knowing full well that in the aftermath of the 2016 elections, what I had assumed would have been a culmination of half a century's worth of aspirations is in many ways more along the lines of a reckoning. But one of the gifts of time is that I have learned that there is a difference between serious introspection and self-pity, as well as between acceptance and complacency. It is no mere coincidence that wisdom, too, has grown from seeds planted that exciting, heady, tumultuous milestone year.

As I look back at 1969, I remember the colorful cast of classmates, agitators, and hangers-on who populated my life at the University of California, Berkeley, in awe of the amount of heavy lifting we attempted regarding multiple social, political and personal issues ripe for transformation. I arrived at UC Berkeley as a freshman a few years prior, committed to making this a more just world, but not having a clue where to begin. I attended all my classes, advanced through a series of positions on *The Daily Californian*, the university's student newspaper, and played the first clarinet with the band—but I was aware of the growing unrest, not only around me but in my awakening heart. If you were there, you've got to love this anecdote from Jerry Rubin, who was hanging around the UC Berkeley campus around that time:

> "A sunny day on the Berkeley campus. Students are carrying ten pounds of books from one class to the next.
>
> "We nonstudent fuck-ups say, 'Excuse me, student. Did you know that the sun was shining?'
>
> "They look at us like we're crazy.
>
> "We invade the libraries yelling. 'The sun is shining! The sun is shining!'" (*Do It!* Simon and Schuster 1970.)

By the time I was a junior in 1969, I'd begun figuring it out. Assisted by the support of an organically-expanded consciousness, if Jerry were still running around the campus trying to wake us up, I was undoubtedly joining in, taking pride in being as disruptive as possible without getting kicked out. As a columnist en route to elevation to arts editor at *The Daily Cal*, I had an amplified platform from which to critique whatever I could get my hands on, from sexist fraternities and oppressive professors to the Vietnam War. My academic department, Communications Studies, took a dim view of my critiques. I wasn't the only one speaking up. Things got so increasingly out of control on campus, by the time 1970 rolled around, graduation had to be canceled at the last minute, forcing students with upset parents in tow to pick up our diplomas from the department offices. I recall that instead of being congratulated by the dean, I got reprimanded.

The year 1969 was also when I met my husband Dan atop a scaffold at a rock and roll concert in a warehouse, the Hell's Angels serving as security and my husband part of the psychedelic light show crew. My parents didn't approve of their college junior dating an ex-sailor fresh from Vietnam. He had wasted no time throwing his uniform into the trash, joining a band and growing his hair long, and for both of us, it was love at first sight. Dan represented freedom, itself, to me. I was tired of conforming to my parents' expectations and instead began to ask what it was that I wanted for myself? This young man had all the attributes I valued—curiosity, kindness, creativity, courage—and if I had to go through the pain of being disowned because he didn't measure up to my parents' expectations—so be it. I chose wisely—survived the period in which both parental funds and affection were withheld—and initiated, in dramatic fashion, the twin spirits of independence and love that have been the hallmark of our life together for 50 years.

It would be no surprise in this retelling that 1969 was also the year I took an elective as part of my UC Berkeley coursework titled "Freedom," Political Science 101X. Because the course boasted a stellar faculty, hundreds applied to enroll, but only 25 got in. The experiential class was supposed to allow students to explore the meaning and experience of freedom, culminating with making a film based on our discussions.

In a class called "Freedom," students continually attempted to relate to one another and the subject matter authentically while professors insisted on analyzing, abstracting, killing whatever students proposed. The professors then proceeded to do what they had wanted to do in the first place. One wrote the script, one directed, we students relegated to bit parts in mob scenes, and carrying cameras and props. Rumor had it that the film was finished and installed in the university archives, but only the professors had seen it, and at any rate, most of us had already quit the course.

Just as I rebelled against my parents' expectations of marrying somebody acceptable to them, so did I relate to my college education, resisting the pressure to conform to some pre-fab model of success, determining, instead, to emerge "a vital human being." Late in '69, I wrote an article, part-confession, part-advice, sharing the method to my revised version of success: "The most important thing we can learn here is how to work the system. For instance, plan to take your least favorite requirements in spring quarter, counting on student walkouts, teacher strikes, and tear gas wafting in from the quad to cancel your classes. Take that time and do something more meaningful with it. And if you need the credit to graduate, you can always work out a deal with the professor to take the course pass-fail. You'll be free to invest your time doing things that matter."

Aside from dodging riots en route to my job at *The Daily Cal*, what did I do with my wrested time? I embarked upon my real education, planting and nurturing the seeds of a life worth living. In addition to initiating and deepening my relationship with Dan, I read, thought and wrote a lot about my values. After escaping my tear-gas-filled Telegraph Avenue apartment following the explosive protest at People's Park, Dan and I went north to take long walks on the beach. We talked about what we wanted out of life, the changes in society we knew were necessary. Exposing myself to spiritual writings from many eras, regions, and traditions, I began to challenge the internal as well as external constrictions that had previously limited my thinking.

Of course, challenging boundaries in search of expanded freedom is not without its risks, and so it is that 1969 was also the year I made a bad choice, but that as time would tell, turned out for the best. My commentaries on student life running in *The Daily Cal*, despite enraging the chair of my department, were winning national attention. *Mademoiselle Magazine* thought it would be great to have someone on the edgier side join their highly-publicized class of a dozen or so interns from colleges across the country who would spend the summer of '69 on staff in New York. At the time, the magazine was all Peter Pan collars and lip gloss, and I was, well, there's no other way to say it. My idea of dressing to impress was to don a lime green Sergeant Pepper uniform from a local thrift store. And my idea of entertaining was to invite the editor, who had flown to Berkeley from New York specifically to interview me, to a pot party. She was not impressed. When I got the rejection letter, I felt torn between the belief that my parents had been right all along—that I felt doomed by my insistence on doing things my way. But on the other hand, even back then, I had the suspicion that getting on track to a big job in New York City was, while the epitome of something, not a true reflection of my aspirations. Instead, the summer of 69, I bought a cheap backpack and headed to Europe where, among other adventures, I found myself sitting at the feet of Krishnamurti in the foothills of a mountain in Switzerland.

Fifty years, a doctorate in religion from Vanderbilt, and thirty books of my own later, I am swept anew with an appreciation for how the choices—even the foolish ones—I made that one year so determined the entire course of my life. Often over the many years since, I have continued to do my best to live according to my authentic core and values. Of course, I had no idea how challenging this would turn out to be. Just as back in 1969 I sometimes confused the pursuit of freedom with knee-jerk reactivity, so have I at times conflated compassion with acquiescence. Moreover, I thought I would not make the same number of mistakes as did my parents; that I would always know the difference between right and wrong, and always, once discerned, have the courage and conviction to act upon it. As someone who has taught university-level students about ethics in experimental courses at Pepperdine and Georgetown, among others, I suppose that there must be at least a few films about freedom gathering dust in the archives somewhere.

It is easy to look back now and realize how alternately ungrateful and naïve I was about both the gifts and challenges of living a life of privilege in America on a college campus circa 1969. But mostly, I admire the breadth and depth of our cohort's vision: what we hoped and fervently believed we could do better than those who came before. I thought that the seeds we planted back then would have grown into something grand and transformative by now—the better society we thought we had under our belts. Instead, I have come to appreciate that my greatest contributions have come about on a far more modest scale, one apology, one act of kindness, one adept communication, one act of forgiveness at a time. At 70, with seven decades under my belt, I find myself feeling exceptionally tender towards it all, less a case of nostalgia than of gratitude, for the 20-year-old who, above all, committed to living life to the full, come what may.

As I write about 1969 in the year 2018, I am clear that these last fifty years have made sense after all: that going for what matters most, succeed or fail, is in and of itself the fulfillment of some higher purpose. In fact, what matters most about 1969 is the same thing that matters most about the entirety of life: that the seeds of a life worth living can be planted, nourished and harvested whatever age one happens to be and whatever the circumstances with which one is faced at any given time.

So yes, Jerry, you were right. The sun was shining back in 1969. And half a century later, still is.

CHAPTER THREE

The Black Armband

By Brent Green

Reverend Doctor Henry G. Bart, dean emeritus of the Kansas School of Religion, decried the Moratorium to a sympathetic crowd of locals and military personnel gathered in a city park. "They are attacking servicemen and ridiculing what has been accomplished by soldiers from this city and those across the country." His face became flush with anger as he paused to drive home his point and absorb approving applause.

"Today's radical demonstration of pacifists and rebels will be an attack on us," Bart continued. "It will be an attack on what we stand for, what we have always stood for and America itself. I can tolerate appropriate policy disagreements, but there should be a line drawn between dissent and treason."

As unobtrusive spectators, Buffy and I observed Bart's answer to the Moratorium, his "patriotic ceremony," as he called it, that had been hastily organized to preempt a massive campus-wide protest march that would begin in a few hours.

His voice trembling with passion, Bart added, "And today's dissenters are stepping over the line as are those radicals wearing black armbands to protest the war. They are stepping over the line. Shameful!"

So, what's the problem with a black armband, anyway?

President Franklin D. Roosevelt wore a black armband following the Japanese attack on Pearl Harbor during the morning hours of December 7, 1941. The unprovoked aerial bombing claimed 2,403 American lives, and 1,178 were wounded. The Japanese also sank eighteen ships, including five battleships. All Americans killed or wounded had been non-combatants because Congress had not formally declared a state of war between the U.S. and Japan.

An unassuming piece of black fabric affixed on Roosevelt's left arm solidified national outrage and collective mourning over so many soldiers lost during malicious air attacks. America, the "sleeping giant," awakened, mourned, and prepared for world war. Although the black armband symbolized national mourning and resolve, the president wore it to commemorate the death of his mother, Sara Ann Delano Roosevelt, who had died 90 days earlier. The significance of the president's black armband took on larger proportions as he signed House Joint Resolution 254, a formal declaration of war.

On December 16, 1965, three teenage students wore black armbands to school in protest of the United States' commitment to the Vietnam War. The protesting teens included John Tinker, age 15, his sister Mary Beth Tinker, 13, and a family friend, Christopher Eckhardt, 16. The teens were then suspended from their schools as severe punishment for disobeying approved district policies.

The children's fathers filed a lawsuit with the help of the Iowa Civil Liberties Union. The U.S. District Court upheld the policy set forth by the school board prohibiting students from wearing black armbands. On petition, the U.S. Court of Appeals for the 8th District arrived at a tie vote, which meant that the District Court's decision would stand. The plaintiffs persisted with their suit despite a low probability of success. Known as

Tinker v. Des Moines Independent Community School District, the case was finally argued before the U.S. Supreme Court in November 1968.

On February 24, 1969, the Court favored the plaintiffs with a 7-2 decision that defined the constitutional rights of students in U.S. public schools, specifically the right to free speech. In its landmark decision, this Court concluded that a black armband represents "symbolic speech" and therefore must be protected under the free speech provision of the First Amendment to the U.S. Constitution. Justice Abe Fortas, who wrote the majority decision, declared that students don't "shed their constitutional rights to freedom of speech or expression at the schoolhouse gate." Known as the Tinker Test, the Court's judgment is still applied to assess whether a school's disciplinary actions or prohibitions concerning matters of speech violate students' Constitutional rights to free speech.

Almost nine months later, on October 15, 1969, Buffy Barrett brazenly displayed her black armband, much to Dean Bart's obvious consternation. He had seen her in the crowd and pointed her out, rendering this gentle co-ed an object of mob derision. Boos showered us with revulsion. "*Nasty KU hippies,*" someone yelled. "*Traitors,*" yelled another.

Buffy took calculated risks as did any college student who shamelessly displayed his or her politics in a time when the nation's divisions had fostered confrontations, beatings by police and civilians, and disgusted glares from those who rejected student disobedience as nothing more than immature imprudence. The Tinker siblings received piles of hate mail following their 1965 suspension. Someone flung a brick to shatter a window of the family car. Another would-be terrorist threatened to bomb their family home.

A skirmish involving stunning Buffy was unlikely, even in the tense situation created by a religious leader, since she would remain in the protective cocoon of a liberal college campus, populated by bellicose activists, joining thousands of others—

students, community sympathizers, and faculty—who could no longer remain neutral or passive about an undeclared war in Southeast Asia. A war with escalating American troop deployments and concomitant fatalities.

As we walked to a patch of open ground where I intended to snap some portfolio photos of this beautiful woman, I glanced at Buffy's black armband and considered Bart's sentiments about her suddenly fashionable accessory. "Bart is stirring deep and hateful resentment among those who believe in the American Way—"

"His way or the highway," Buffy insisted. We continued walking in silence, bewildered that such an icon of campus religious education could be as close-minded about mushrooming antiwar protests at this university and across the nation.

She posed for my camera, allowing me to snap a series of photographs. My tool was a popular Japanese camera, a Mamiya/Sekor 500dtl single lens reflex. While this camera was not failsafe, it nevertheless took some of the guesswork out of exposure and shutter speeds, allowing me to concentrate on my subject: a captivating co-ed who wore a black armband as more than just a fashion statement.

My camera brought grand simplicity to the task of capturing her nuanced intimacy with history in the making. Proud and defiant, she posed with fists on her hips, a sense of righteous indignation blending with seductive allure. She was twenty years old, beautiful, popular, and boldly willing to wear her political convictions tied around her coat sleeve.

The bright October sun that late morning cast her shadow on the park lawn, creating dimension and solidarity. Her dark brown eyes exuded intelligence as they met my camera lens. An experienced fashion model and dancer at a local nightclub, her outfit was form fitting. She wore a big city winter coat, woven with intricate patterns of wool and fashioned like a Navy pea coat, short in length, broad lapels, a double-breasted front, large wooden buttons, and slash pockets. Though fashionable and expensive, her coat also looked rebellious, augmented by an armband that the highest court in the land had sanctified as an inviolable demonstration of symbolic free speech.

Buffy and I did not know we were capturing history in those few moments of creative collaboration. War protests on college campuses had become commonplace by the fall of 1969. But this day would become the largest peaceful protest of the war in American history and would be known as The Moratorium to End the War in Vietnam or just the Moratorium.

President Richard Nixon railed against this day of protests during a press conference: "Now, I understand that there has been, and continues to be, opposition to the war in Vietnam on the campuses and in the nation. As far as this kind of activity is concerned, we expect it; however, under no circumstances will I be affected whatever by it."

Nixon had few friends on college campuses. He had promised "peace with honor" as he campaigned once again for the presidency in 1968. Voters elected Nixon in part because of his promise to end the war. In 1969, however, his administration expanded the war. Even though college students always doubted his veracity, at least he had tossed a bone to the antiwar minority among voters. This day, October 15th, would bring many more citizens into the antiwar movement, spreading from high schools, colleges, and universities to Main Street, America.

I felt a sense of exhilaration as Buffy and I walked twenty minutes from the city park near 5th and Alabama St. to Strong Hall, the epicenter for the forthcoming antiwar rally. Classes had been canceled for this chilly Wednesday. As we passed rows of Victorian houses, many structures unkempt from years of student rentals, we greeted comrade protesters, some of whom were playing rock 'n' roll albums and drinking beer on their front porches.

From a half block away, I could hear melodious harmonies of The Temptations singing the number one song on The Billboard Hot 100: "I Can't Get Next to You."

Kansas skies were brilliant blue with a crisp chill in the air as we trudged up the hill to the Oread neighborhood. We encountered hundreds of students, radicals, dope-smoking hippies, revolutionary foot soldiers, and a smattering of brothers from the Black Student Union. We felt animated by the drama of unfolding civil disobedience, the pressing moral duty to stop an unpopular, deadly war, even if it meant exile and condemnation from Nixon's "silent majority."

"My father rejected me this past summer," said Buffy. "He's a well-known Chicago attorney, and his politics fall to the right of Spiro Agnew's—"

"Agnew disgusts me," I interrupted.

"I know his politics are anathema to our views," said Buffy, "but why do you despise him?" She was a chip off the old block when it came to acting confrontational and not accepting comments on face value.

"He's unhip ... straight ... bull-headed, with hard-hat, working-class male machismo."

"My dad has met the vice president. Dad says he's dapper, self-made, a non-Ivy Leaguer, tightly disciplined, powerful, and quiet."

"Quiet? You're kidding. I'd call his demeanor aggressive and snarling."

Buffy grabbed my hand and squeezed. "He has a way with words, thanks to his speechwriter, William Safire. Did you hear Spiro accused the war opposition of being an 'effete corps of impudent snobs who characterize themselves as intellectuals'?"

"I may be effete, but I'm not snobbish about this nationwide antiwar protest. The poor and undereducated are more likely to be drafted and fighting in Nam. It's not a war for any senator's son and anyone in the inner circle of this vice president. My impudence springs from a determination to end this war now."

Buffy relented, "He's the number one dude among the William Buckley crowd."

"Yes," I agreed. "And God help us if he ever becomes president. He's more Nixonian than Nixon, more of a hardliner on race relations, fighting in Vietnam, and on the scope of executive power."

A hippie woman approached us from the direction of the Kansas Memorial Union. In her hands, she grasped several black armbands. She sized us up and recognized that I was not wearing an armband. "Here, hon," she said. "You should match your lovely partner. You need this symbol of mourning and protest."

"Why is that?" I said.

"I can see that you're thoughtful, intense, and a longhair. That's good enough for me."

I took an armband from her outstretched hand. Buffy helped me tie it above the elbow of my right arm. "You're a stunning lady, thank you."

Standing on her tiptoes, she kissed my cheek. She spoke to Buffy. "Let's get our brothers out of Nam. Let's stop any more from being shipped over to that jungle graveyard."

"Let the world see and hear what we feel about this war today," said Buffy. "Won't you join us?"

"I'm a nurse and due back at the hospital," she said. "I took my lunch hour to give away as many of these armbands as I could find takers. Nobody has turned me down. I had more than a hundred when I started my campus tour. This is all that remains. Peace!" She abruptly walked away.

Something stirred deep within me, and I shouted after her. "I love you, sister."

As we neared the Union at noon several minutes later, thousands had already gathered. Students skipping classes. Professors agreeing to give back one day of salary because they refused to teach during the Moratorium. A handful of hippie drifters passing through Lawrence. Locals. CIA suspects. Cops. Brothers from Lawrence High School. The mood was hopeful but intense.

The stirring crowd began a marching parade along Memorial Drive. Chants inundated through the throng, a creative variation of the school's famous mantra at sporting events: "Rock chalk, Jay Dove. Stop war, try love!"

At Strong Hall, the crowd paused, then numbering more than 5,000. In an orderly row stood 150 students, each person standing behind a wooden white cross. The reminder of death took on palpable dimensions.

Never shy in a crowd, Buffy joined in with others who began singing an antiwar anthem recently performed and made popular by John Lennon and Yoko Ono.

All we are saying is give peace a chance
All we are saying is give peace a chance

A loud and large member of the KU football team stood on a bus bench, towering over the crowd and yelled, "Are you listening, Nixon?"

All we are saying is give peace a chance
All we are saying is give peace a chance

The football player shouted louder, "Are you listening, Agnew?" The horde cheered his boldness as he spoke with conviction. "War hawks claim that only a minority has been conducting a campaign to stop the war. They believe our motives are suspect and self-serving to avoid the draft. They see us as cowards."

The multitude erupted again in catcalls and boos. The football player held up his hand to beseech them to calm down. "Listen to me! The hawks believe our judgment, loyalties, and patriotism are questionable. They believe our actions today border on treason!"

Cheers and loud applause echoed from Strong Hall and other limestone buildings surrounding the thousands of us who would not remain silent.

The jock continued. "The real political problem with this Moratorium isn't the 'usual troublemakers': radicals, hippies, revolutionaries, disenfranchised students, and anarchist professors." Giggles and catcalls waved across the crowd.

"Listen to me! Other people such as our Chancellor, local business leaders, and prominent politicians have stepped forward to instill this day with respectability and patriotism. We are winning the battle to capture the hearts and minds of Nixon's 'silent majority.'"

And then I saw his black armband jump to the foreground of my awareness, presenting a striking and definite contrast with his urbane leather letter jacket. I glanced at my armband and felt a deeper connection to all those who stood with me in defiance of Nixon, Vietnam, and undeclared war. I took Buffy's hand, glancing at her black armband, visualizing the photos that would soon be developed, printed, and then stored in a photo album entitled *1969*.

This truth survives with Buffy's black armband photo: We passed the Tinker Test and had been granted a constitutional right to be seen and heard.

CHAPTER FOUR

A Report from the Scene

By David Cogswell

Unfortunately, when Rodney got into the service, it turned out it was not a good fit after all. It was like an irresistible force meeting an immoveable object. His relentless defiance of authority did not sit well in the military service. And he was incapable of giving up his independent volition, knuckling under and taking orders.

Nineteen sixty-nine was the year I left my youth behind. I had left my childhood behind much earlier. When I was seven, after my father left my mother, my sister and me for another woman, I remember my mother stooping down to my level, looking me in the eye, straightening my collar, and bucking me up to go outside. "You know you're the man of the house now," she said. It was the late '50s. That was the moment I woke up from the childhood dream.

I adapted quickly to my elevated status; growing up with a single working mother I became very independent. My mother constantly struggled to make ends meet. As a working mother, she was gone much of the time, and I was on my own. During the day she would go to her job, and in the evenings, she was often busy with her social life. She was an attractive, single young woman and didn't wish to remain single forever.

Being on my own suited me. I had plenty of ways to entertain myself. I enjoyed rich, solitary pursuits, reading books, listening to music, playing piano, drawing pictures, writing confessions, poems or songs, watching a few choice TV shows. I inhabited a world of my own. It was a cloistered life.

I had a very limited view of the outside world. I saw newspapers and heard the news on TV and radio, but only superficially. For the most part, I inhabited my little world while the events of the wider world streamed by as if in a dream.

History Unfolding

What I knew of American history was what I had learned in school. I learned the values all Americans were taught then, at least I thought so. I learned that America was a free country and a champion of freedom and justice throughout the world. And communism was the opposite. And the Nazis were also the opposite of America, and the opposite of communism too.

In the summer of 1960, I tuned into the Democratic Convention on TV and witnessed the rise of John F. Kennedy, who went on to win the election and become the president of the United States. Even though my father was a vehement Republican and portrayed Democrats as evil people, I found myself irresistibly drawn to Kennedy and the sense of dynamism he brought to the country. Liking Kennedy was my earliest glimmer of independent political thinking. I was eleven when Kennedy took office in January 1961.

Suddenly the revered President Eisenhower, who seemed to be a very old man, was swept into the past along with the whole world of the 1950s. Like a flash of lightning, the electric '60s had begun. The world had changed. But although Kennedy's energy radiated powerfully enough to reach me in the hinterlands of Kansas, my political awareness was primitive. Only the top veneer of political news filtered down into my private adolescent world.

Then in November of 1963, when I was 14, came that horrible day when everything changed again fundamentally. The dashing young president who had brightened our landscape and inspired us with a sense that a greater world was possible was wiped out—obliterated and suddenly gone.

It was a horrendous nightmare thrust upon our country, a murky, grisly affair, as if the lowest depths of the underworld were suddenly thrust onto the center stage of our political and cultural life. It was hard to make sense of what we were told about what was happening.

One did not have to be politically aware to be deeply moved by the violent destruction of the handsome young president, who left behind a beautiful young wife and two small children. It was a deep trauma experienced at once by a nation of 190 million. Grief radiated around the world.

Dreams Killed and Reborn

Suddenly our dream world of the '60s, with all its promise, its vibrant colors, and energy that had so completely differentiated it from the '50s, exploded and vanished, "like a dream that fades into dawn." We seemed to have been swept back again into the dark and gloomy past.

And there was Lyndon Johnson, big, heavy and slow, with greased-back hair and sagging jowls, lumbering up to the microphones at a podium on a runway after he emerged from Air Force One just after being sworn in as president.

He opened his mouth and drawled out a few slow, ponderous words in his heavy Texas accent: "This is a sad time for all people," he said. "We have suffered a loss that cannot be weighed. For me, it is a deep personal tragedy. I know that the world shares the sorrow that Mrs. Kennedy and her family bear. I will do my best. That is all I can do. I ask for your help—and God's."

He spoke mechanically, not sincerely. But he was right about one thing. It was a loss that could not be weighed, and never can be. Our brilliant young, charismatic, dynamic president was gone. The whole scene changed in an instant.

But all the inspiration Kennedy had churned up could not be instantly dissipated. It had to be transmuted, re-channeled. And it was. After a period of collective grief, that spirit would stir again and seek new avenues of expression.

A few months later, many in my generation found a new focus for our visions for a new world in four charismatic figures from England. The Beatles represented some of the same qualities of youthful energy, freshness, optimism, grace and cosmopolitan intelligence that were part of the Kennedy mystique.

As the youth culture of the 1960s grew and coalesced, the Beatles became the de facto leaders of a cultural revolution. Like the frost patterns on a windowpane, once the required catalyst was in place, the new consciousness crystallized and spread across the country almost instantaneously.

The world had changed. The cultural revolution gathered momentum and mass and spread rapidly through the country. It was an exciting time to be a teenager.

What I had no clue of then, but which would soon throw the country and my life into turmoil, was the war in Vietnam, which was about to flare from a flicker to a ferocious blast.

Trouble Across the Sea

I learned decades later that, soon after Kennedy's death, President Johnson reversed an executive order signed by Kennedy to begin withdrawing troops from Vietnam.

Kennedy had lost faith in the mission in Vietnam. The U.S. had been entangled there since the early '50s when the French tried to reestablish their colonial hold on the Southeast Asian country after World War II, meeting such fierce resistance that they were forced to abandon the mission. The U.S. stepped in to bolster the old order and got stuck.

Kennedy had built up the number of U.S. "military advisers" in Vietnam to 17,000. But he had come to see the government of South Vietnam as corrupt and at odds with its people. He decided to wind down U.S. involvement.

"In the final analysis, it's their war," he told Walter Cronkite, in a filmed interview. "They're the ones who have to win it or lose it. I don't think that the war can be won unless the people support the effort, and in my opinion, in the last two months, the government has gotten out of touch with the people."

In the first week of October 1963, Kennedy issued an order to begin a phased withdrawal of troops, starting with bringing 1,000 troops home by the end of 1963, with the withdrawal to be completed in 1965.

The withdrawal plans were not made public at the time because it was politically and strategically sensitive. But Defense Secretary Robert S. McNamara acknowledged it in his memoirs. Other historians, including Arthur Schlesinger, Peter Dale Scott, and John M. Newman have told the story as well. So, sadly we learn that something else we lost when we lost Kennedy was an early exit from the horrors of the Vietnam War.

Johnson committed himself to do whatever it would take to avoid being the president who "lost Vietnam." In July 1964 he ordered 5,000 more troops to Vietnam, and on August 2 there was allegedly an attack on a U.S. ship in the Gulf of Tonkin. In the hysteria whipped up around the incident, Congress passed the Gulf of Tonkin Resolution, giving Johnson the power to conduct war without a declaration of war.

It turned out that the alleged attack hadn't happened. But the Gulf of Tonkin incident became the pretext for escalating the war, which went on for another ten years, killing 58,000 American soldiers and an unknown number of Vietnamese before finally being given up as a lost cause.

Youth Culture Collides with War

But back in my world when I was in high school, none of this was even considered by anyone I talked to. I was set to graduate in 1967, the Summer of Love, and it was a thrilling time to be coming of age in America.

Youth culture was flowering in beautiful ways. Our popular music had undergone a metamorphosis and become much more exciting, colorful and energetic, embodying a world of new possibilities. The arts and fashion flowered with an explosion of new, more colorful styles.

But my trajectory, and that of my generation, was about to collide with much darker historical movements taking place at the same time. From my point of view, practically everything coming out of the blossoming youth culture was exciting and novel. But in the background, a killing machine was roaring.

The rapid acceleration of the war effort was ramping up as I graduated from high school and reached the age when I had to sign up for the draft. At that point, the American war effort was escalating at a dizzying rate.

Here's how fast it accelerated. In 1963 there were only 122 American casualties in Vietnam. In 1964 there were 216. Then the number of deaths began to increase by orders of magnitude. In 1965 the casualty number jumped to 1,928. In 1966 it jumped again to 6,350, and in 1967, my graduation year, it soared to 11,363. Almost a thousand young Americans were getting killed every month in Vietnam. And the numbers were still growing.

This was the world I stepped into when I graduated from high school. I was not aware of any of this until I got into college and had to sign up for the draft, which every young man in America was required to do when they turned 18. Mandatory military service brought the carnage of the war home to the streets of America.

For my graduating class of 1967, which was in the Pentagon's direct line of fire for their personnel requirements, it crashed down on our world out of nowhere. We were broadsided.

We had no idea what it was about, or why 19-year-olds were being forced to give up their lives, their careers and their dreams to become killers of people in some distant country we had never heard of. The politicians said it was to stave off the Communist threat, but that seemed remote and abstract. It didn't ring true for us. We didn't feel like our leaders were honest with us, and our mistrust grew.

Fathers and Sons in Conflict

With the war building to a boil, those of us who were of draft age had to make our life decisions with that in mind. We were told we had an obligation to give ourselves up to be pawns for some military man to order into battle. But for what? What was the reason for all this?

What was happening to me was happening to millions of young Americans across the country, and it set off a massive social upheaval. It changed our relationship with the government overnight.

Suddenly we were plunged into existential choices. We were told our lives were not our own, that we had to give up our plans and our lives and obey the orders of men in Washington. But there was no clear threat.

If America had been under attack, most of us would have rallied and joined the fight to defend it as our fathers' generation had. But that wasn't it. Something wasn't right about it. For my generation, it broke down our trust in authority. But our parents' generation was still living in the mindset formed in World War II, when our country, our allies, and democracy itself were under attack, and the enemy was clear and unmistakable.

My father's attitude toward the war in Vietnam was the attitude he had formed in World War II. But that was a very different war and a different world. And my generation responded to it very differently. And the society became bitterly divided along that line.

When Politics Comes to You

When I arrived at Kansas University in Lawrence as a freshman in the fall of 1967, the campus was a hotbed of political activity. Political activism was roiling, and information was everywhere. It would have been hard to avoid. And since these issues affected my life directly and urgently, I became politically galvanized quickly.

The more I learned about the politics behind the war, the more I questioned it. I soon came to see it as an immoral war and believed the only moral stance was to oppose it.

Unfortunately, the World War II generation didn't see it the same way. It was only 20 years since the end of that war, and to them, it wasn't long ago. For us teenagers it was like ancient history. The principles they were dealing with then didn't apply to our situation.

I found myself firmly aligned with the antiwar movement. Because so many people were getting killed, it made the issues very intense. These were not abstract discussions of arcane policy decisions. It was life and death. And I was in the mainstream of the population that was getting shipped off to Vietnam. We all had to decide what to do.

I was eligible for a college deferment. But I felt guilty about that because others whose parents couldn't afford to support their college aspirations might have to go and die instead. It was very confusing.

I was tormented by all the moral ramifications, as were millions of others. Some acted out their confusion and frustration in tragic ways. People I knew engaged in a variety of self-destructive activities, from overuse of drugs to one friend who shot a military officer in the act of blind rage and ended up in a mental institution. We also had our casualty list here in the United States.

It seemed like there was no good way to deal with it. How does one individual go up against such a mighty, giant machine? It was a question a whole generation was asking.

Though I wanted to oppose the war, I didn't want to go to jail. I resolved that at least I would not let them force me to be a killer. I participated in some anti-war demonstrations, but there was a sense of futility about it. Later I learned that the demonstrations did help to end the war. But I didn't know that then.

I didn't know what to do. For the moment I just stayed in school, biding my time till I could figure out a better course of action. But my conscience tormented me. It seemed that nothing I could do could satisfy my conscience, resolve the contradictions, and soothe my sense of moral outrage.

A wartime mentality set in, the sense that whatever you're going to do, you'd better do it, because tomorrow you might be dead. I dived in with wild reveling and drug taking, smoking pot, and exploring LSD and speed. The wildness spread through the culture like wildfire.

Things just seemed to get wilder and wilder. In a short period, my country changed into something unrecognizable. It was boiling over with conflict. There was unrest on the streets of America. Everything seemed to be coming apart.

In the summer of 1968, as the anti-war movement built, the war became the issue that defeated the incumbent president in the New Hampshire primary. Suddenly there was new hope. LBJ withdrew from the race, and it looked like Bobby Kennedy, who advocated withdrawing from Vietnam, might become president.

But then in April, Martin Luther King, the civil rights leader and resounding voice of conscience, was murdered in Memphis. Two months later Robert Kennedy was murdered in Los

Angeles. It was a tumultuous and violent time. The shocking news was flying too fast to comprehend. It seemed as if violent forces were defeating all opposition to the war in America.

Then came 1969, the pivotal year.

Losing a Friend

That spring, my friend Rodney came to visit me at my apartment in Lawrence. His father had been a career army man, and he had not been groomed for college. When I went to KU, he had stayed in Topeka and taken a factory job.

In junior high and high school, we had been like brothers. For years we spent a great deal of our time together on practically a daily basis. We rode to and from school together. On the weekends we went out running around like maniacs with our small circle of friends. We spent endless hours during the summer days boxing, teaching each other how to defend ourselves by beating each other up. We had been very close through junior high and high school. It was sad and strange to see our paths in life diverge.

Rodney told me he had decided to join the army. It was incongruous because he was hands-down the single most rebellious, anti-authority person I had ever met. He defied any attempt of anyone to tell him what to do. At that time, he had come to terms with going into the military by thinking of it not as an act of compliance but rather as an adventure. He was going into helicopter flight training.

I held back my feelings of sadness and wished him the best of luck. Soon after that, he was in the army. I heard from him through a friend who exchanged letters with him after he left.

Unfortunately, when Rodney got into the service, it turned out it was not a good fit after all. It was like an irresistible force meeting an immovable object. His defiance of authority did not sit well in the military service. He was incapable of giving up his independent volition, of knuckling under or taking orders.

He had always been all about the dare. He would dare to do things almost no one would do. But he would not let anyone tell him what to do against his will.

It came to a head at a big military event that the generals attended with their wives. Rodney got drunk, and as he stood in the inspection line, he unzipped his pants and took a pee. It was a level of defiance that could not be tolerated in the military. It was an affront, an insult that would have to be met with the most severe consequences. This time he was up against something much larger and more lethal than he had ever encountered during his youth.

Oh, you want to play games with us, little boy? You have no idea what you are up against.

It was over for Rodney. His career track was wiped out. He was pulled out of helicopter flight training, dropped into the infantry, sent to Vietnam. Within 30 days he was dead, killed by American supporting fire.

It was as if my brain blew a gasket. I was more disillusioned and enraged than ever against the establishment of my country. By then my whole generation was reeling and rolling with the punches, which seemed to be flying faster and faster.

Some members of my high school class had a grim reunion at Rodney's funeral. I had been one of his closest friends for years, and his parents knew it because they saw me at their house all the time. But they didn't want me as a pallbearer because I was wearing my hair a little longer than before, marking me as a member of the counterculture, and the enemy.

The divisions were deep and bitter. Rodney's parents were, of course, heartbroken, but part of their rage at losing their son was directed at people like me who were on the other side of the great divide.

I was deeply demoralized and embittered. My world seemed to be getting torn down piece by piece. Now the war had really come home, taken one of my best friends, and then turned his parents against me so we couldn't even share our grief. Our greatest leaders had been killed. I didn't know what was left. My generation was worn out.

That summer the biggest ever pop festival in history was planned near Woodstock, New York, and I hitchhiked with a couple of friends to New York. We tried to attend but the rain fell hard and heavy, and the traffic became so clogged we got stuck and ended up hanging out in New York.

In the fall, I went back to school to begin my third year of college. That semester I met a freshman woman who stole my heart and turned me around completely. I made the commitment to forsake all others, threw my lot in with her and was swept away into the trials and tribulations of marriage. I turned my back on all my past.

It was the end of 1969. The '60s were over. The Beatles had broken up. The war dragged on like a huge machine running on inertia. Counterculture members were tired and disillusioned.

With the death of Rodney, the last vestige of my youth was gone. My idealism, my simplicity, my belief in the principles on which I had been raised. America passed out of the '60s as abruptly as it had come into them. And there we were in the dust and rubble of it all, trying to figure out where to go from there.

The 1970s stretched out before us as an unknown frontier.

CHAPTER FIVE

Double-Crossed

By Brent Green

When Baby Chick pulverized Jackson O'Leary because Jackson wore a Christian cross around his neck, I didn't fully grasp my moral anger. I was mad—seething. The man Rick and I had long admired for his achievement of a black belt in karate—my college roommate—well, he had piled up in a greasy parking lot, his face covered with blood. He writhed painfully, semi-conscious and disoriented. Baby Chick strutted as a crowing rooster, calling him foul names, threatening to send him from the asphalt to an emergency room. Chick's acolyte Custer held a knife near my stomach, daring me to interfere and promising to filet me if I did. Rick, our other roommate, stood next to me frozen with dread. His eyes darted from Custer to me to the knife to a cheering crowd, back to Jackson and Chick. Where this story is heading began more than a decade earlier.

I had developed a tentative relationship with Christianity during childhood—a Sunday thing partitioned to a boring day each week when nothing happened except duty. We were a proper American family, nicely groomed and socially aware worshipers. We attended Sunday school and church, respected the yawning drudgery of "family day at home," and relished Mom's ten-course dinners.

Icons of the church created visceral anxiety that I labored to bury out of conscious reach. I had an ambiguous appreciation of church doctrines: original sin, final judgment, rapture, salvation, and a far-off future when my transcendental spirit might reside in heaven or hell. Once I even experienced a flash of divine love, summoning self-conscious tears.

Mostly I remember Catholic imagery, although I was not Catholic but a meeker Protestant. Bruce Cox, my boyhood friend and next-door neighbor, had been raised excessively Catholic, and he showed me photographs of liturgical paraphernalia and crucifixion paintings that had seemed graphic and specific about inevitable death experiences. I still see the Son of God suspended on a cross and an anatomically perfect heart glued to His torso as a decal. That image caused wonderment and disgust.

I remember the Congregational church sanctuary where I had spent many hours sitting next to my parents. A gold-toned cross, spanning two stories, hung above the sanctuary. To escape the drone of the preacher's sermons too conceptually complex for my young mind, I studied the details of the metallic surface. I thought about its shape, its rectilinear edges, its material, how it had been mounted to a brick wall, and what would happen if it fell on the choir below. Changing its appearance to suit my imagination, I saw it ignite with flames as if a gas stove burner: dull blue light would encircle the cross, flames would transform into lightning bolts, and the cross would then lift away from the wall to float above a pious congregation. Sometimes Christ would materialize as a vision, and all those Sunday believers would gasp with the arrival of His manifestation. I thought about my physical body lifting from a pew and floating up to become part of the crucifix.

Those fantasies of power and divinity would cause my pulse to race. The sanctuary cross became my way to escape monotony and weight of being both young and mortal. It had raw iconographic power, but not for the right reasons—at least for the reasons proffered by our pastor. Nevertheless, motivated by boredom's imagination, I gave the symbol careful respect.

One momentous Sunday I had dressed in heavily starched olive-drab clothes with a bright red bandana tied around my neck. My heart pounded in anticipation for my moment of glorification. Sitting next to me, my parents seemed frozen with hopeful anticipation. We had been separated near the front of the church with other parents and their sons, also dressed in olive-drab uniforms. About halfway through his service, the minister summoned us to stand next to him. We lined up stiffly near the lanky spiritual leader.

He spoke about us in glowing language. He talked about our sacrifices: long Saturdays spent laboring under his direction, polishing obscure nooks of the church. He talked about arduous undertakings to memorize Beatitudes and The Lord's Prayer. He proclaimed that we were exceptional examples of teenager dedication to traditional values: mother, father, church, God, and country. Then he pinned medals to our Boy Scout uniforms.

The pin had been crafted from cloisonné melted on brass; a red serif cross lanced a pure-white background. The shield hung from a chevron of shimmering blue nylon. It glowed with hot pride on my chest, red and white righteousness—a flag brandished by early Christians in pursuit of heathens. My face burning with humility and awkwardness, I saw an enthusiastic congregation watching their sons. When the minister finished, parishioners applauded our achievements. That is what stands out—I had never seen or heard people clapping during a church service. It had been unexpected, something akin to Christ materializing on a gold-toned cross hanging above us.

I maintained silent attachment to that symbol of my determined journey to the God and Country Award, not so much for what it symbolized—an emblem of faith—one of the Boy Scout's most difficult awards to achieve—but because it has lingered as relevant years later, a rare experience when I felt flooded with sweet joy from my parents' homage. The medal became my private symbol for achievement and uncomplicated holiness.

Jackson could not even roll into a fetal position to protect his torso from further physical abuse by Baby Chick. Jackson's shoulder-length red hair had become matted with sweat and blood from a gaping cut above his left eye. Chick and his gang laughed at Jackson's defenselessness.

"Come on," Custer challenged, "go ahead and jump in there."

I looked past his sneer at my injured roommate, and I felt the adrenaline surge through me. My legs hardened; my heart raced; my fists coiled into tight balls. Rick must have sensed my readiness to take up the challenge. "Don't. These guys have us outnumbered."

"This college boy has some brains," yelled Chick to the crowd. "You want to see 'em spill?" Several men from the 3.2 beer bar yelled encouragement. I felt mounting alarm as the stocky man continued to circle Jackson. He raged as if a two-legged bull. His stubby legs pounded up and down as he stomped his pointed cowboy boots next to Jackson's ears. "Com'on hippie, get up and show us you're a *real college man.*"

I stared in simmering disbelief, my anger primordial.

That Friday night had rolled out harmlessly. Rick and Jackson and I were jovial when we met at The Wheel in Lawrence. An early spring day invited us to choose to play over studies. College girls were wearing less and less, and the bar near campus had been packed with happy, TGIF-ready co-eds. I arrived first, and then Rick showed up about four-thirty. Jackson strolled in at five o'clock. The bar overflowed with guys from fraternities and girls from sororities and a smaller contingency of hippies. Long hairstyles and bohemian clothes had quickly become a popular fashion among the disaffected and revolutionized. We felt we had gained an emerging sense of attractiveness to sorority women. They stared at us more than they did when we had short haircuts and wore fraternity pens and V-neck sweaters. We returned to The Wheel on Friday afternoons to scout for amorous adventures and to slug down some beers. Jackson tumbled into the booth next to Rick. Something novel and out-of-place hung from his neck: a gleaming gold cross about the size of a half-dollar coin. Prior experience suggested that Jackson wore it to make a fashion statement, not because he had decided to demonstrate newfound born-again consciousness.

"Are you transferring into the School of Religion?" I began.

"Yea, Jackson, it looks like you're a priest or something," Rick added.

Jackson chugged from Rick's glass. "Found it in my stuff last night. I got it after catechism. Looks pretty cool with this black turtleneck, doesn't it?" Slender but strong and possibly dangerous, his posture suggested confidence and surliness. His eyes poured over us, deep brown and determined, and his round cheeks moved with hundreds of freckles. His strawberry-blonde hair had grown longer than mine, and more artfully wavy, soliciting compliments from nubile young women.

"Sort of cool," I offered. Remembrances jumped through my mind of a sanctuary with brick walls and a giant gold cross, suspended above, and my Dad's prideful radiance.

Continuing our typical roommate pimping, Rick said, "We're not going to mass tonight, I hope."

"No more crap, guys," Jackson said. "This is kind of a peace symbol. Don't sweat it. What are you dudes up for tonight?"

I shrugged and glanced at a buxom blond as she pushed through tangles of students by our booth and then studied Rick. "Too many damned decisions this week. What do you think?"

Rick's ice-blue eyes followed my blond quarry as she walked away from us. His black curly hair hung as filigree around dark cheeks. His angular face, pointed nose, and somber eyes often attracted attention because of vague similarity between his face and that of Paul McCartney of The Beatles. Given the immense popularity of the British rock 'n' roll band, Rick had an automatic rapport with women. His eyes refocused upon me, and he seemed to understand my question. "Well, I have an idea. Let's go to Topeka."

"Topeka!" Jackson said. "You've got to be kidding. What's in Topeka worth a trip?"

Rick said, "There's this bar on Huntoon Street. Several people told me it fills with women on Friday nights. We've never been to Topeka before. Why not? Have any better ideas?"

I shrugged again. "This college town gets to be a drag, a predictable Friday routine going nowhere and leading to a Saturday morning hangover." A fully endowed brunette pushed by our table, and we became transfixed for a moment. Lack of further comment about a Topeka trip constituted a decision.

We stayed at The Wheel long enough to finish a pitcher of Bud and then another. Since the beer contained scant 3.2 percent alcohol, we rarely felt more than a gentle buzz, but it provided enough alcohol to loosen our spirits and fill our minds with endless possibilities of an unscripted Friday night. Jackson and Rick did most of the talking because I felt solemn and reflective. I studied the gold cross around Jackson's neck, and I felt trepidation; although it could be thought of as a piece of jewelry, it grew expansive in its message. It hung obtrusively around his neck, and it glowed with defiance and inexorable power. Frat-rats passed our booth; one guy after another glanced at the bangle around his neck. It begged for attention, and I felt self-conscious. Jackson seemed relaxed and easy; I assumed he felt nothing but pride and typical cockiness.

We drove old Highway 40 to Topeka in my Volkswagen Beetle. By then it had become dark outside. A two-lane highway took more driving time than the Kansas Turnpike, but the old blue highway, lacking congestion, felt mellower. The thirty-minute drive gave Rick enough time to light a joint, which we passed back and forth. I had a couple of tokes but refused any more; I hated getting too stoned while driving and then trying to maintain in a socially chaotic situation. We chatted about existential philosophy and the Vietnam War. A male bond hardened between us that exceeded college boundaries and the coincidences of our shared apartment. We complemented one another.

Jackson busied himself as an intellectual explorer. He devoured books on philosophy and psychology. He experimented with meditation to expand awareness through body-mind control. He had been practicing karate for several years. He would perform exercises in our living room and demonstrate the raw power of concentration and channeled physical focus. He loved to appear from nowhere and thrust a side-kick at my groin, stopping short of nailing me.

Rick served as our rock star, although he couldn't play a musical instrument, nor could he hold a tune. The coincidence between his appearance and Paul McCartney's precipitated his affinity for rock 'n' roll. He decorated walls around his bed with photographs of the *Fab Four*. About that time, the Beatles' *White Album* had hit the charts, and Rick played it hundreds of times. He listened for coded messages, rotating the album backward on an LP turntable, memorizing the lyrics. He dressed in British mod clothes. On this day he wore pinstripe bellbottom trousers, a blue chambray dress shirt with blossom sleeves, a wide leather belt, and black dress boots. When he met a sultry coed, and she made the psychic connection between his appearance and McCartney's, his speaking style would then take on a distinctively British flavor. He smoked Benson & Hedges cigarettes with theatrical flourishes.

I became the link between Jackson's physical/spiritual worldview and Rick's rock-star persona. Studious and serious about graduating, I added a circumspect, earthbound dimension to our living space. During weeknights I would retreat to my books, reading my assignments then devouring non-assigned books by Herman Hesse and R.D. Laing. Rick and Jackson would often tempt me to break my monastic vows of careful scholarship, but I would rarely oblige. When they became carried away with teasing each other, I would intercede with a sober voice of sudden maturity. Once they nearly wrecked our apartment during a pillow fight, and I had to tame their zeal with exhortations of personal responsibility.

A pugnacious swarm filled the parking lot next to Bambino's Bar. Several men jumped on car roofs so they could get better views of the fistfight. Incandescent streetlights filled the area with a dull orange glow. Still prone on the asphalt parking lot, Jackson managed to push up on one elbow, and he shook his bleeding head in disbelief.

Somebody shouted from the crowd. "The dude's had enough."

Chick swung around to assail this bystander with a barrage. "But you ain't calling the shots, pussy. Maybe you want to take this freak's place?"

The peacemaker self-consciously pulled back. A woman tugged his arm, and they left the area.

We had reached Bambino's at about eight o'clock. This dive was unfinished inside and smelled of stale beer and body odor. Young people packed the place. Women constituted a decisive majority, so Rick had been correct about that prognostication. As we walked through the door a jukebox blasted a new Conway Twitty tune. Rockers at heart, we hated old country music, but Rick shrugged and pushed through the crowd by maneuvering towards the bar. One thing became apparent: we were the only men with hair long enough to reach our shoulders. I felt conspicuous as a sudden minority. Jackson also seemed aware of our alternative appearance, and he stiffened, exuding cockiness. Rick became transfixed by an expected majority of comely young women.

I caught a few alluring glances, but Rick discovered a young Beatles fan. This petite blond did her thing as a surrogate groupie, and Rick provided a stimulus for her adulation. Let's face it: you wouldn't expect to discover a real rock star at Bambino's in Topeka, Kansas, so Rick represented a reasonable facsimile. Jackson furrowed his eyebrows and fastened his unrelenting stare at potential adversaries. He appeared uncomfortable with the atmosphere of this bar, and I found it easy to agree with his body language. We were out of place. We would have left earlier if Rick had not found a flaxen female to seduce with his British accent. The noise level in the bar had been manipulated so piercingly that Jackson and I found it difficult to chat, so we just drank our beers and anchored ourselves to the bar.

Rick gave it his best shot. I must admit: the girl did send out the right signals. Leaning close to him, she fed him plenty of sensuous eye contact. As he talked about himself—his favorite topic—she pushed her full chest closer and closer. It seemed destined when he proposed a liaison. "My roomies and I are heading back to Lawrence. Do you wanna take a ride, doll?"

The pretend groupie froze, no longer warm and pliable. "I'm Baby Chick's chick," she said.

Perhaps she had teased him beyond the point of sensibility, but he replied with a lack of discretion in his choice of words. "Babe, any guy named Chick must be a turkey." He put his arm around her waist and nudged her to come hither. "Where is this Chick, anyway?"

She pulled away and nodded toward a single pool table on the opposite side of the bar. Under the spotlight of a hanging Budweiser lamp, a compact man stretched over a green felt table, pool stick in hand. He wore a white T-shirt and baggy blue jeans. His arms were enormous for his size, clearly a weightlifter. His greasy blond hair had been combed back into an out-of-style ducktail. A cigarette hung from his lower lip. Rick stiffened. "So—that's Baby Chick!?"

People will normally act according to expectations. Sure, there are occasional aberrations, but somehow, we find a way to place unexpected, unscripted behaviors into a comforting context. Maybe we revise our expectations. Maybe we become a little more guarded, but we still view the person from a durable perspective. My roommates and I didn't know that bantam blond lady, but she seemed normal on the surface. With Rick, she did a very juvenile thing by teasing and goading. You expect this kind of behavior when you enter a bar filled with young adults getting loaded on watered-down suds. However, she seemed to be ready to play. Nothing about her attitude had prepared me for what happened next.

"This freak's hitting on me, Chick!"

She didn't merely speak these off-putting words: she screamed them. Bambino's denizens froze as if some off-stage director had said, "Quiet on the set."

Then she severely scolded Rick. "You're like every college hippie I've met. You think you've got brains, and high school chicks want to screw!"

I stared across the room at Baby Chick.

The scene evolved in slow motion. As if an actor in an old black and white movie, he tossed his pool stick on the table. He stuffed his cigarette in an ashtray and yanked his jeans over his beer gut. His eyes riveted on Rick and, as if he'd started traversing the Red Sea, onlookers parted to create a path between Chick and Rick. Jackson set his beer on the bar and swung around to face Rick and this nemesis. Chick sauntered toward Rick and stopped within inches of his face. I'm sure Rick would have backed up if the crowd behind him had not created an impenetrable wall.

"Are you messing with my woman?" Chick demanded.

Rick shrank although he towered over Chick by three or four inches. "Not really." As bright as Rick could be, he sometimes failed to pick his words carefully when under stress. "She didn't claim you until I asked her on a date—"

"You asked her on a date!" Chick pressed, yelling. He grabbed Rick's shirt and lifted him up on his tiptoes. Jackson stepped forward.

"Let him go," Jackson said in an unruffled tone.

Chick didn't let go of Rick's collar. He looked at Jackson and said, "Are you this freak's mother, or what?"

"Just let him go," Jackson repeated.

Chick released Rick's shirt slowly. "Are you his mother, mother-fucker?"

Jackson stepped closer to Chick. "She was coming on to him. It's not his fault."

Someone from the crowd taunted, "Kick the hippie's ass, Chick."

Images of three bashed and beaten longhaired college students filled me with dread. I could see this event coming to no constructive conclusion. Moving closer, I said in a loud voice, "We're splitting. This thing isn't worth pursuing."

Rick looked at me with relief. "Yea, you're right. Let's blow this Popsicle stand."

Chick was not satisfied. He looked again at Jackson, who had not allowed his eyes to waver from his adversary. Chick grabbed for the cross hanging around Jackson's neck. "What's this cross shit? Are you one of those hippie Jesus freaks?"

Jackson then used a simple karate move, grasping Chick's pudgy fingers, and pulling the intruding hand away. Pain winced across Chick's face.

"You dumb-ass freak!" Chick yelled. "Step outside."

Jackson acted disinterested. I, on the other hand, squirted enough adrenaline for the three of us. My heart pounded, and I felt self-conscious about bar-fly eyes staring hatefully at us.

"You will lose," Jackson said.

"Oh yeah? Well get your hippie ass outside, and we'll see about that," Chick said.

Jackson walked through the parting crowd with ease, Chick followed; Rick and I followed the rooster, and the crowd pushed behind us.

I had no doubts about Jackson's mastery of karate. The only problem with this method of fighting is embedded civility. People square off politely; there's always an acknowledged beginning—a courteous bow; the fight culminates with another obeisance. And Jackson performed the martial arts as much for spiritual nourishment as for self-defense training. Chick, a street brawler, understood and respected only one thing about fighting: clobber the opponent as fast as possible.

As Jackson walked through the exit, Chick hit him on the base of the skull with a closed fist. Jackson stumbled forward dazed, and he swung around to face a barrage of quick and hard punches from Chick's flat fists. Jackson never had a chance to move into graceful and practiced motions of a karate master. This bout had become a street fight. Under more managed circumstances, I'm convinced Jackson could have bashed the ungainly brute, but Jackson was mentally out of it before the bell for the first round. Three naive college students discovered that street-fight culture does not have standards for civilized conduct. Jackson demonstrated several effective blocks and even landed a sharp jab on Chick's chin, but he could not regain control to establish superiority.

Rick stood still next to me, eyes wide and glassy. He yelled encouragement. "By God, smash his face, by god—hit him!"

I evaluated the situation. It seemed that Jackson might regain the upper hand if Chick could be distracted for even a few moments. I stepped forward with a vague plan to jump on Chick's back and hold his arms for as long as I could. As I made my move, another short and stocky man brandishing an open pocketknife pushed next to me.

He said, "Mr. Custer suggests you stay out of it." The knife wasn't particularly threatening as knives go, but five or six guys standing behind him were unquestionably menacing. I held back and watched Chick beat Jackson to the ground.

Far off in the background, I heard wailing from several police sirens. Most of the crowd rushed back inside Bambino's, but Chick remained, undaunted, circling Jackson and badgering him. To my relief a few seconds later I saw blinking red lights zooming toward us from about a block away. Chick saw them also, so he stepped back and let loose a final, full-tilt kick into Jackson's back. Jackson yelled in anger and pain. Chick leaned over and yanked the cross from Jackson's neck, speaking softly. "If I ever see you again, I'll shove this goddamn cross up your ass. Got it?"

Jackson said nothing in reply, his quiet defiance a sign of courage rather than disorientation. He had become a mannequin, unmoving, unemotional.

As two police cruisers arrived, Chick and his cohort charged back into Bambino's. The police officers tried to make sense of this scene, but Jackson refused to give them any information other than he had been beaten in a bar fight. His bloody face swelled into a freak show.

"Who did this to you?" a cop insisted. "What happened?" Jackson remained stoic.

Another officer looked at Rick and me. "Who beat him up?"

Just as I felt prepared to spill the entire story, Jackson caught my glance, a nonverbal message loud and clear: he wanted no further complications with the law.

"I got here too late to see the other guy clearly," I answered. Rick nodded agreement.

A thwarted investigation ended with a lecture by an older officer. "You college kids should stay in Lawrence. You don't belong in Topeka. You hippies come here and cause trouble." He looked at me and added, "Can you drive him?"

"Sure," I said, "I've only had a couple. He's my roommate."

[49]

The officer checked us out again, as I considered a small plastic bag of righteous weed under my car seat, the imminent possibility of a narcotics search. Perhaps the officer thought we had had enough trouble for one night, so he let us go without further questioning or intimidation.

Jackson acted disoriented. I suggested a hospital, but he resisted the idea. "All right," he said, "just get me home." I recommended that stitches might be necessary for a gash above his left eye. He said again, "Damn it—all right. Just go home now." Rick and I helped him into the back seat of my VW.

While I drove the empty county roads back to Lawrence we did not speak, shell-shocked. I glanced over my shoulder several times at Jackson to make sure he did not go into a coma, or worse. Flat on his back, his legs doubled-up at the knees, he stared emptily at the ceiling of my car. I felt betrayal, surprise, shame, and fury.

Back at our apartment building thirty minutes later, we helped Jackson into his bedroom. His face had become grotesquely swollen. It was obvious he would have a serious shiner. I wet a washcloth so that he could wash dried blood from his face. Rick and I tried to minimize the beating and tell Jackson we supported him.

"You guys watched me get my butt kicked," he said. "There's nothing more to it than that. Let me get some sleep!" He flipped onto his stomach, burying his head under a pillow.

Several hours later I woke from a restive sleep. I had been dreaming one of those chase dreams where the bad guys are after you, and you are running away as fast as you can, and your legs don't move fast enough. Just as the bad guys grab for your legs, you wake up. Moonlight streamed through windows above my bed. I remained still for a few minutes trying to clear my head of awful mixed feelings about surreal fight dreams and the reality of an injudicious bar brawl. I heard shuffling noises from our living room.

Cracking open the door to my bedroom, I peered into grayness and saw shadows reflected against a wall next to our kitchen. I edged into a hallway and rounded a corner leading into the living room. Light from a single candle flickered. Two dark figures sat on the floor facing the candle. They appeared to be reading from a large book.

"What are you doing?"

Rick spun around. "We're reading the Bible, man. Jackson woke me two hours ago. We've talked about life and death and then we started reading this Bible." He turned back to the book. Jackson said nothing.

I was uncertain about what I should do, so I sat on a couch and watched them for a few minutes. They ignored me. I could not contain my curiosity any longer. "This is kind of weird, don't you think?"

Jackson twisted and evaluated me; his distorted face had become freakish. I felt compassion for his pain. He said, "Jesus also suffered. He was ridiculed and flogged and eventually crucified—the passion of the Christ, man.

"For a long time, I have felt empty of spirit. Now I am full. What once mattered is no longer of consequence. I *deserved* to get my royal ass kicked; my lesson—the waste of violence. Now I cherish peace." He returned to the Bible and became absorbed with reading.

Rick acted hyperactive in comparison to Jackson's contemplative mood. "Yeah, man, we just had a religious experience. It's never happened before. We were talking about tonight, and suddenly a sense of calmness filled us. I've never felt this way before. Jackson understood it immediately. He said, 'The Holy Spirit has come into our hearts.' I didn't believe him. But as we talked, I knew he was righteous. It was my idea we should read the Good Book by candlelight. Cool, huh?"

I no longer recognized my roommates. They had changed—a raw, atavistic clarity in their perspectives, a newfound reverence, and humility. I sensed they would never be the same as they were. I had lost familiar parts of my roommates in a parking lot outside Bambino's, Topeka's brutal Coliseum. I tried to share their feelings, but I could merely comprehend the situation objectively as if this religious moment had become part of a made-for-TV movie and me, merely a popcorn-munching spectator.

"The part about tonight that I regret most," Jackson added, "is that Chick stole my cross. I never understood its power until Chick ripped it from my neck." He hung his head, and I felt him sobbing. The three of us had never shared that emotion before.

"Yeah, it was the work of the devil. Chick is Satan," Rick added. He bowed his head and wept.

I jumped from the couch. These improbable events trounced me with confusion and raw respect. "Excuse me," I said, feeling like an intruder.

I shut my bedroom door, flipped on an overhead light and paced my room. My thoughts churned with images of violence and religion. I fought this paradox for an hour. I saw Chick's fists smashing into Jackson's face again and again. I saw the Congregational sanctuary from my childhood Sundays—iconographic images, Renaissance paintings, pious weekend worshipers. And in an instant, I saw an image that would render all this mystification manageable. The answer I sought had been hidden for years in a corrugated box, at that moment stored underneath my bed.

I dug into the box and tossed memories onto my bed: my first baseball glove, an empty wine bottle from senior prom, a stack of love letters from Sandi, baseball cards, a photograph of Elvis, a few semiprecious gems left over from a rock collection, my high school yearbook, and, finally, the object of my search. I uncovered my Boy Scout God and Country award wrapped in a red bandana. I tore the blue nylon chevron from the cloisonné cross then rummaged in the box until I found a discarded brass chain. After attaching the cross to the chain, I cautiously opened the door. By then Jackson and Rick had returned to their bedrooms. I knocked softly on Jackson's door. Hearing no response, I eased his door open until light from my bedroom landed on his face. Profoundly asleep, he did not budge. His right arm extended beyond the mattress with his hand cupped upward. I tiptoed to his bedside and placed my award into his outstretched hand. His fingers reflexively closed, and he clinched the Christian cross in a firm fist. My cheeks burned with humility and mortification, as on that remarkable Sunday during adolescence when I had been granted an award for questionable, incomplete faith.

Jackson wore that cross every day for the rest of the school year, his righteous crusade pure and provident.

CHAPTER SIX

The Peak of American Civilization

By Richard Adler

If history teaches us anything, it is that every civilization, no matter how glorious and powerful, eventually falls. But the greatest civilizations at some point reach a peak of accomplishment that endures and contributes to the story of human advancement. The Egyptians erected the pyramids. The Greeks built the Parthenon and invented democratic government, while the Romans established an unparalleled empire and built many engineering marvels. England, at its high point, created a truly global empire and balanced monarchy with parliamentary power.

The United States in its relatively short reign as a global superpower has been the source of many important innovations, starting with its Constitution through inventions such as the telephone, the electric light bulb, atomic power, and the computer. But I believe that its most historic accomplishment, one that will represent our civilization's high point, took place in the summer of 1969.

I vividly remember the moment that it happened. On the evening of July 20, 1969, I was attending a party at a house in Portola Valley, California, a few miles north of Stanford University on the San Francisco Peninsula. I was very aware of what was about to happen that night, so I brought along a battery-operated portable Sony television. As the historic moment got closer, I set up the TV on a table next to the home's swimming pool. Before long, a group of other partygoers gathered around the set's tiny black-and-white screen. For the next hour, we watched in awe as Neil Armstrong and Buzz Aldrin brought their lunar lander down on the surface of the moon and then watched Armstrong as he descended the ladder from the craft and took the first human step on the moon.

It was indeed a small step for a man but a giant leap for mankind. For the first time since life arose on this planet, one of its creatures—an American—had left Earth, ventured into space, and walked on the surface of another world.

Of course, this was not an overnight accomplishment. The space race that motivated this journey began in 1957 when the Soviet Union put its Sputnik 1 satellite into orbit. This accomplishment shocked Americans and spurred the United States to accelerate its activity in building rockets. In January 1958, just four months after Sputnik, the U.S. put Explorer 1, its first satellite, in orbit. That fall, President Eisenhower signed a bill that created the National Aeronautics and Space Agency to pursue "the exploration of space."

For the next several years, the U.S. had to work hard to keep up with the Soviet Union. In April of 1961, the USSR put Cosmonaut Yuri Gagarin in orbit, making him the first man in space. It took nearly a year for the U.S. to equal this feat, finally launching John Glenn into orbit in February 1962.

But the most important event in the race to the moon came later that year when the country's young president gave a speech on September 12 at Rice University in Houston, Texas. John Kennedy began his speech by putting what he was about to say in a very long perspective. He started by recapping 50,000 years of human history by condensing it to "a time span of but a half-century." In this framework, he explained, "we know very little about the first 40 years...only five years ago, man learned to write and use a cart with wheels. Christianity began less than two years ago. The printing press came this year, and then less than two months ago, the steam engine provided a new source of power." He ended this account by noting that "only in the last week did we develop penicillin, television and nuclear power."

He then said that considering this "breathtaking pace" of invention and progress, some might want to pause and rest. But Kennedy rejected that notion and committed the United States to immediately undertaking "one of the great adventures of all time." In the most famous words in his speech he explained that "we choose to go to the moon in this decade...not because [it is] easy, but because [it is] hard." He then went on to enumerate just how formidable the challenges would be to accomplish this audacious goal:

> We shall send to the moon, 240,000 miles away from the control station in Houston, a giant rocket more than 300 feet tall, the length of this football field, made of new metal alloys, some of which have not yet been invented, capable of standing heat and stresses several times more than have ever been experienced, fitted together with a precision better than the finest watch, carrying all the equipment needed for propulsion, guidance, control, communications, food and survival, on an untried mission, to an unknown celestial body, and then return it safely to earth, re-entering the atmosphere at speeds of over 25,000 miles per hour, causing heat about half that of the temperature of the sun—almost as hot as it is here today—and do all this, and do it right, and do it first before this decade is out.

President Kennedy concluded by emphasizing that to accomplish all these things, "we must be bold."

The effort over the next decade was bold—and costly. Several astronauts died in preparing for the lunar expedition. In 1967, NASA's budget, most of which was devoted to the Apollo program, peaked at $5.9 billion, which represented almost four and a half percent of the federal budget (today, NASA accounts for less than one-half of one percent of the federal budget).

I got an opportunity to get a first-hand look at just how massive and far-reaching the effort to get to the moon was. In the late 1960s, I was a graduate student in English at the University of California at Berkeley. This being the height of the '60s, Berkeley was a lively place. But in the hills that rose west of the campus, far above the tumult taking place down below, was the university's Space Sciences Laboratory, built with a NASA Facilities Grant and opened in 1966.

Despite my lack of scientific training, I managed to get a job as the lab's librarian. To get to the lab, I would wend my way up Strawberry Canyon, behind the main campus, past the football stadium and the university's botanical garden to the building that was situated in a eucalyptus grove at the very crest of the East Bay Hills. On many days, I would drive through a thick fog that covered Berkeley's lowlands and drive out of the fog just as I reached the top. Working in the lab's library sometimes felt as if I were flying—I could look out over the top of a thick fog bank and occasionally be able to see the Farallon Islands some 30 miles west of the Golden Gate.

I soon discovered that a big part of my job as a librarian involved unpacking and shelving large cartons of books which arrived regularly from NASA, most of which were filled with esoteric things like calculations of the orbits of the earth and the moon. Although I grew up loving books, I had to admit that these volumes were totally inscrutable to me.

One day, a large semi-trailer arrived at the lab to deliver a new piece of equipment. It was an ultra-high-resolution mass spectrometer that filled an entire room and had been airfreighted from the UK to Berkeley, along with a team of British technicians who spent several days installing the machine. One of the grad students working in the lab confided to me that one of the lab's senior researchers (a Nobel Prize winner) had convinced NASA that this device would be extremely useful for analyzing rocks that would be brought back from the moon. But in fact, the researcher wanted the instrument to study the Australian tar sands that were the focus of his current interest.

In addition to keeping many faculty members and grad students employed, I hope that the work accomplished at the lab, including my humble contribution, did contribute in some way to the success of the Apollo program.

As awe-inspiring as the 1969 moon landing was, it was soon followed by a letdown. The moon turned out not to be a very interesting place, just a bunch of rocks and sand not very different than what can be found on earth. The last manned landing on the moon came just three years later with Apollo 17.

And back here in the U.S.A., things weren't going that well. When the Apollo 11 astronauts splashed down in the Pacific after returning from the moon, they were greeted by President Richard Nixon, who would soon bring us Watergate. The Vietnam War dragged on. The 70s were also notable for the oil shock, hyperinflation, and the Three Mile Island nuclear power plant disaster. Succeeding decades brought Reagan and Reaganomics, the AIDS epidemic, the spread of PCs, mobile phones and the internet (which seemed like great innovations at the time, but are increasingly seen as problematic), 9/11 and the start of a seemingly endless war on terror, the opioid crisis, and, most recently, the presidency of Donald Trump whose vision of heroic action is limited to building a wall to keep immigrants out of the country, and is otherwise intent on fomenting division in the country and undoing as many environmental protections and social advances as possible.

The past few years have made me question whether my deep and largely unconscious belief in the inevitability of human progress is true.

Through all of this, the saga of exploration of space has continued. But humans have not ventured very far from earth since our last visit to the moon. The U.S. built the Space Shuttle to make travel into space more routine, but it was only designed to orbit the earth, and the program ended after the Challenger exploded soon after launch in 1986 and the Columbia disintegrated on re-entry in 2003. Today, the only humans in space are the few inhabitants of the International Space Station, which travels around and around the earth at an altitude of fewer than 300 miles.

Instead of humans, it has been robots that have been doing the exploring beyond earth. Robotic probes have cruised by all the planets and given us detailed views of their surfaces and of their surrounding moons, which may be the most interesting objects in our solar system (some, like Saturn's icy Europa and Jupiter's volcanically active Io, may harbor extraterrestrial life). We've even made close-up visits to several asteroids. The Curiosity rover, which reached Mars in 2011, is still moving around the surface of the Red Planet, while in 2018, the InSight probe landed on Mars to explore its geology. And the Hubble Telescope has provided astonishing images of deep space for nearly 30 years.

Perhaps America's most remarkable venture in space has been the two Voyager probes, launched in 1977, more than 40 years ago, and still moving outward and sending messages back to earth. By the end of 2018, Voyager 2 was some 11 billion miles from earth and was traveling at about 34,000 miles an hour. In December, its instruments signaled that it had left the "heliosphere" of solar emissions and had entered interstellar space. On board of Voyager, along with its scientific payload, is a record that NASA describes as "12-inch gold-plated copper disk containing sounds and images selected to portray the diversity of life and culture on Earth" that was included just in case the probe might be found someday by an extraterrestrial who would be curious about who sent this object into space.

There is still talk of humans getting back in the business of exploring space. But these days, it is led by visionary entrepreneurs like Jeff Bezos and Elon Musk (who seems to be committed to taking humans to Mars). Alas, this won't happen in my lifetime.

In some distant future, when the history of the 20th century is written—perhaps as a single chapter in a much longer story, perhaps in a book (or some yet unimagined medium) written on a distant planet—one event that certainly will be included is the moon landing of July 1969. Even if America's great civilization has declined or disappeared, this accomplishment will remain as its signal contribution to our human story, and I'm glad that I was here to witness it.

CHAPTER SEVEN

Cat's in the Cradle

By Brent Green

Vietnam would be a virtuous and commendable place to die at age 19, ripped to shreds by a Bouncing Betty or blown apart by a Soviet 7.62mm AK-47 assault rifle.

Not!

I harbored few vestigial heroic fantasies about paying with my life for a one-way ticket to those steaming jungles. More U.S. soldiers died there in 1969 than any other year except 1968. In April, the number of American military personnel stationed there peaked at 549,500. A detested war had become way too popular at The Pentagon.

I had a blessed student deferment, but true freedom required more if I was going to take a break from college, get a job, and save some money for a much-anticipated backpacking trip throughout Europe. I also needed a break from pressures of committing to a college degree that had lost meaning—at least a semester off, or better, a year—but to do that required a deferment with perpetuity, one that guaranteed liberation from involuntary induction no matter where my wanderlust and I should traipse.

Before the war became a political and cultural nightmare of epic proportions, I had tried to do the right thing according to military aficionados by signing up for ROTC during my first semester of college. I concluded that if I had to fight in that war—and from the lens of a crazy year, it seemed inevitable that I would—then the only intelligent way to ship over to Southeast Asia was as an officer. So I thought.

The idea of being a second lieutenant seemed more reassuring than arriving as a grunt foot soldier. With officer status, I might have position and rank and be more likely to avoid deadly fighting. Perhaps I would become staff support to a high-ranking officer. Or type boring forms all day. Or maybe reorganize supplies that had already been reorganized. Something worthy of my intelligence. I might not even hear and smell that war, safely ensconced on an army base far away from lethal action. These considerations all seemed reasonable at age 19. I did not know then that American officers were the preferred POW bounty sought by North Vietnamese Army combatants.

I retain gauzy memories of learning to march in formation in front of Allen Fieldhouse at the University of Kansas. First came stationary drill commands, requiring minimal coordination but imposing much anxiety, a gift that kept on giving from the domineering drill sergeant. Eventually, the sergeant issued forward march commands that, directed at a bunch of freshman grunts like us, must have looked pathetic compared to professional soldiers. We practiced and got better, but far from the benchmarks set by West Point cadets at their worst.

One day after another humiliating, demeaning, confidence-diminishing drill class, the instructor took me aside to inform me that I had been officially kicked out of ROTC. My medical history had finally arrived as required, and there was no place in the army for a cadet with bronchial asthma. My childhood had caught up with me, and indeed I admitted with some relief that molds and ambiguous pollutions of jungle war could kill me faster than a Viet Cong bullet might.

That military decision had no bearing on my status as a prospective draftee should I lose my student deferment. I was at the beginning of my college journey with four years of student deferments ahead. If I stayed in school, took the requisite number of college courses each semester, and maintained at least a 2.0 grade-point average, no problem.

Nevertheless, this tenuous grasp on a student deferment haunted me as it did other college men, realizing that political leaders could change the rules at any time. Politicos could eliminate college deferments altogether. Or they could change criteria by raising the grade-point average students must maintain to qualify for deferments.

Asthmatics? Send the grunts induction letters anyway!

Permanent security rested with an assignment of a magical alphanumeric known as 4-F, a U.S. military classification that a registrant is "not acceptable for service in the Armed Forces due to medical, dental, or other reasons."

The liberating 4-F classification was not easy to obtain, given the unpopularity of the war and a need for so many troops. But many draftees found imaginative ways to dodge induction into the military once a student deferment no longer applied. For example, Donald J. Trump received student deferments during college. Although draft offices assumed a skeptical attitude about medical claims, the future U.S. president insisted he had bone spurs in his feet that would prevent him from passing a physical examination. The man who would become president and Commander in Chief escaped Nam with a medical malady as preposterous as his contemporary blonde-orange comb-over trying fruitlessly to hide a balding pate.

Former Vice President Dick Cheney, a noteworthy hawk who helped lead the nation into wars with Afghanistan and Iraq, was a member of the exclusive "five deferments" club. Following four years of college deferments, he wedded immediately.

Married men of draft age received some latitude concerning the draft, but when they had children, they were liberated from concerns about being shipped off to Club Vietnam.

Less-fortunate sons had to find more resourceful ways to become members of the elusive 4-F fraternity. Those with friendly doctors might obtain letters from their physicians identifying medical conditions likely to win deferments. But this method was hardly foolproof. The military had its doctors, all guided by conservative policies that thwarted feckless diagnoses such as "anxiety disorder." Military docs were universally suspicious of letters from family doctors, except apparently a diagnosis of bone spurs applied to a prospective inductee with the last name of Trump, who at this writing wiles away typical weekends on his many private golf courses. (Here's hoping those bone spurs haven't condemned him to the anguish of persistent slices.)

One of my college friends successfully faked hearing loss. The Army used a tone test requiring subjects to listen for a tone and then push a button when the sound became fully muted. He had memorized the sequence of tones with the help of another hard-of-hearing friend, thus creating the impression of consistent tone deafness in certain required tone ranges. Failing the hearing test was an awesome path to rejection, not requiring self-mutilation or humiliating demonstrations of psychosocial pathologies.

I heard about several college dropouts who had lost their student deferments and then claimed mental defects. Convincing military doctors that you were too crazy to be inducted was a high bar to hurdle. However, one of those guys peed on the floor while stripped naked for his physical. He apologized profusely to the examining physician and then fell to his knees and licked his pee off the floor while shaking as if someone having an epileptic seizure. Another guy stripped for his physical and was wearing adult diapers, which had already received a copious dump of feces. Then another dude groped the examining doctor with a seductive come-on; homosexuality was strictly forbidden in the military during the Vietnam War era. Another story may be apocryphal, but a draft dodger living on a farm near the university used a shotgun to blow off two fingers on his left hand. He was planning to be a rancher and thus didn't feel that ten fingers would be essential for his vocational choice.

On December 1, 1969, the Selective Service System of the United States conducted an infamous lottery to determine the order of call to military service in the Vietnam War for men born between 1944 and 1950. I recall a nightmare setting with me standing in my fraternity chapter rec room with fifty other guys who were also subject to the draft, and all huddled around a small black & white television. The days of the year, including February 29th, had been written on slips of paper and then placed in plastic capsules, mixed up and then dumped into a large glass jar. Capsules were then withdrawn one at a time. The first unlucky number was 258 or September 14, meaning that all those draft-eligible men who were born on September 14 would be first in line for conscription. With the withdrawal of subsequent capsules, my fraternity brothers would cheer, boo, throw up, happy dance, or otherwise express profound emotions. Nobody cheered getting a low draft number. The consequences for fraternity men were less so than for those who did not have student deferments, but a looming threat of "Your ass is mine" felt real and palpable and devastating.

The results of the draft lottery in 1969 won me an unenviable position in line for the obligatory physical examination and possible induction: number 71. I remember a cold, sinking feeling in the pit of my stomach and some sympathetic pats on the back from nearby fraternity brothers. My consternation was grounded. The first 195 birthdates drawn were called to serve in Vietnam during the following year in 1970.

My ass was on the line.

Not long after the lottery, I paid a visit to the family physician who had treated me for asthma from age five. Dr. Cohen was a sympathetic medical doctor because he had lost his oldest son in Vietnam a year earlier. On the other hand, the wise doctor was as ethical as any person I had known growing up. He played by the book. He would not put false or speculative information in a letter to the Selective Service System, and he had not formally treated me for asthma since I departed for college two years earlier. He needed concrete evidence that my asthma was still an acute health problem. He suggested that documented asthma attacks treated at the university's student health center would provide enough justification. He told me this with what could be interpreted as a reassuring wink. Continuing asthma attacks would equal liberation from the gnawing triple threats of induction, Vietnam, and death, which simplified means "a real bummer."

Before I drove out of Dr. Cohen's office parking lot, I had hatched a plan worthy of General Westmoreland, commander of U.S. forces. My asthma had been controlled as I reached my college years, although periodically I would feel a familiar tightening of my chest and an anxiety-provoking inability to exhale fully. For these occasions, I had a rescue inhaler that was primarily epinephrine hydrochloride in an aerosol form. A couple of puffs of the inhaler would soon alleviate the symptoms of an asthma attack. Dr. Cohen needed me to take this up a notch.

I called my friend Linda, who lived about two miles from me, and asked for help. Her brother had been killed in the war, and she was vehemently against the Nixon Administration's empty promises to end the military draft and bring American troops home. She was a willing accomplice, agreeing to loan me her cat for a few minutes. Feline dander always sent me into systemic histamine overdrive.

Two evenings later I donned running clothes and ran as fast as I could to her house. As I reached her home, breathless and sweating bullets, she opened the front door and presented me with Whiskers, her beloved Persian cat. Hyperventilating from the Olympics dash to her house, I rubbed my sweaty face with

Whiskers furry body. The cat seemed to like an unexpected new form of petting, mewling with delight—okay, not delight, but with restrained indifference. Within seconds my eyes had swollen almost shut, and I began wheezing and coughing. There is no substance on the planet that I'm more allergic to than cat dander, especially microscopic skin flakes from a feline with dandruff issues. Couple this harrowing moment with my general distaste for the feline species, and we're talking about mega-aversion, body, mind, and soul.

My clever plan at first amused Linda but seeing me suffering such a severe histamine crisis frightened her, and with an alarming sense of urgency, she pushed me into her beat-up Volkswagen Beetle. Breaking city speed limits, she drove me to Watkins Memorial Hospital just minutes before I would have turned blue and passed out. By the time I reached the emergency room my tongue had swollen, hives had covered my face and arms, I was wheezing and coughing, and my heart raced. I had reached the most dangerous point of exposure to allergens: anaphylaxis, a potentially life-threatening condition. Call it tabby-axis.

In the emergency room, I was barely able to inhale, my face continued swelling, and I began to feel faint from oxygen deprivation. The attending resident physician quickly assessed my condition, administered an injection of epinephrine, and put me on oxygen through a facial mask. This asthma attack was so severe that I could have died—one heck of a price to pay for avoiding death in Vietnam.

In about fifteen minutes my breathing became normal, but the swelling of my face continued. A nurse ordered me to wash my face, arms, and upper torso to cleanse away allergens that might have been left on my skin (cat dandruff). She was unaware of how I had been exposed to Whiskers, just that I had been playing with a cute fuzzy-wuzzy furball. She was quite cognizant of my extreme allergic sensitivity. Nurse Hachette reprimanded me for even getting near a cat, much less picking the animal up and petting the woolly ball of hive-inducing, chest-squeezing dander.

That did it. My emergency was dutifully documented, and the fact of my continuing battles with bronchial asthma had become part of a permanent and verifiable medical record. But one near-catastrophic event was not enough for this OCD draft dodger. The stakes were high, and I didn't want to take any chances.

As much as Linda resisted my plan to repeat my intimate moments with Whiskers, she was even more incensed over the continuing disaster of Vietnam. The number of American military personnel stationed in Vietnam reached 543,000, one hell of a number of potential sacrifices in an undeclared war. Nineteen-sixty-eight had the most casualties of the war in a single year with 16,592 American soldiers dead. But 1969 was second with 11,616 war-related deaths. Antiwar protests on college campuses had reached a very loud and bellicose crescendo, dramatized by protest marches and antiwar rallies almost daily.

I returned to Watkins Memorial hospital two more times. Linda helped me stage a second asthma attack visit, but this time we did not mention Whiskers' role in my severe allergic reaction. We didn't want to raise suspicions that I was intentionally triggering attacks. Who me? That would be un-American. During hospital admission proceedings, I made a vague reference to having tasted a hunk of forbidden dark chocolate, and the same resident who treated me earlier said, "Whatever."

My third visit to Watkins involved another friend, another run across town, and another cat—a giant Maine Coon by the name of Herman. While Herman was not blessed with as much fur as Whiskers, he weighed eleven pounds; there was plenty of him to rub against my face. He wasn't as docile as Whiskers and about ripped my face off with clawed enforcement of personal space. He was in a bad mewed. Ha! Ha! His contrite owner sensed retaliation and grabbed his front paws before he could scar me for life—or introduce the possibility of a severe bonus case of cat-scratch fever. For the benefit of the student hospital record, I attributed the third attack to elm tree pollen, abundant that spring because of significant rains.

Three documented asthma attacks for six weeks constituted all the proof that Dr. Cohen required to write a forceful letter to the local Selective Service System office. The tone of his letter was authoritative and emphatic. There was no way in his judgment that I could successfully serve in the military due to severe and documented allergies to pollens, molds, chickens, chocolate, wheat, and random petrochemicals. My asthma attacks were severe and ongoing even as a college student able to insulate myself from overexposure to typical allergens. His letter did not mention my substantial aversion to cat dander, believing that a military physician could conclude that exposure to housecats would be a nonexistent problem in Vietnam. I might simply assassinate any offending creatures crossing my path during surprise jungle encounters.

Several weeks later a letter arrived at my college apartment, stating succinctly that due to a pre-existing condition—bronchial asthma—I was not physically qualified for military service, and therefore my classification had been changed from 2-S, a student deferment, to 4-F, meaning, "Your dreams of becoming a heroic officer in a man's army will never come to fruition." REJECTED (you cowardly fortunate son).

Cats were never my favorite animals. I even developed creative ways to psych them out (never physically harmful but psychologically ingenious). My cat psych strategies kept away cats determined to mark me by rubbing against my legs with their scent glands. Whiskers and Herman potentially saved my life, doing their feline duty for God and Country, pushing me into severe bronchospasm attacks, protecting my ass for an opportunity to write this overdue confession.

Rodney Wilson, a popular high school classmate, died in Vietnam in 1969. When the war was finally over in 1973, 58,200 Americans also became military fatalities. Like many of my young male peers of that time, I had moments of indecision about the morally correct course of action. Many of our fathers served during World War II and the Korean War, and those who had made the sacrifice received heroic recognition and appreciation from a grateful nation: marching bands, ceremonies, awards, and ticker-tape parades. Our fathers were indeed heroes, sometimes reluctantly, but supermen, nevertheless.

Dodging the draft sometimes felt cowardly, thus my initial attempt to join ROTC in college and rise to the rank of second lieutenant upon graduation. I did not see myself as a duty deserter, but like so many of us back then, the war seemed morally corrupt. The ignoble mission had been packaged with ironclad American values, but the purpose and benefits of the undertaking were never clear or justifiable. History seems to favor the side against that costly war. Even Robert McNamara, Secretary of Defense under both John F. Kennedy and Lyndon B. Johnson, soured on the war long before troops came home in 1973. "We were wrong, terribly wrong. We owe it to future generations to explain why," wrote McNamara in his 1995 memoir, *In Retrospect, on the Management of the Vietnam War.*

Some would argue that I had dodged Vietnam for durable reasons. Alongside me were three American presidents of my generation: William J. Clinton, George W. Bush, and Donald J. Trump. This is not justification, simply facts that the nation must absorb and accept. Or not. I hope our future leaders will understand the differences between justifiable defensive wars and unjustifiable offensive invasions of other sovereign nations where indigenous populations resent encroachment and will, together, fight tooth-and-nail to thwart incursions by foreign invaders. (See: Iraq, Afghanistan, etc.)

As anticipated, I dropped out of college for a semester during the fall of 1970 to reset my priorities, find meaning within all the raging confusion about my purpose in a dysfunctional society, plan an optimum future as a worthy nonconformist, and sharpen my surprising culinary skills. I accepted a job as a maître d'hôtel in a gourmet Italian restaurant, serving politicos, big shots, wealthy patrons, and sordid mafia types, but that's another story.

Bananas Foster, anyone?

CHAPTER EIGHT

Hell No!

By Bob Moses

1969 It was a hell of a time.
Born in 1946, I arrived with the first wave of the Baby Boomers. By 1964 we had added 76 million new Americans to the population. We were born to a generation largely united by World War II, a massive enterprise undertaken by 16 million enrollees in the U.S. armed forces and bolstered by a patriotic home front and a burgeoning industrial war machine that lifted the U.S. out of the remaining dregs of the Great Depression. The economic boom from 1945 to 1969 consolidated our position as the world's richest economy. We, the Boomers, were the world's richest kids.

Beginning my senior year at Hamilton College in Clinton, NY, in the fall of 1967, I had one thing in mind. To get the hell out of Dodge and go where the world was happening, and rapidly leaving me behind. Vietnam. Civil rights. Politics. And, yes, sex, drugs and rock 'n roll. Robert Kennedy visited our campus that fall, decrying the war. Richie Havens, too, belting out the

Beatles' "Here Comes the Sun" and Dylan's "Maggie's Farm," imbuing in each song a more urgent intonation. Dylan spoke for many in the Hamilton class of '68, cloistered up on College Hill and pondering our futures as he sang: "Meanwhile life outside goes on all around you."

I busted out of prison (college!) in 1968, a tumultuous year that saw the beginning of the Tet Offensive in South Vietnam in February, President's Johnson's decision in March not to seek another term, MLK's assassination in April, followed by RFK's in June, and capped by riots at the 1968 Democratic Convention in Chicago and over 100 more U.S. cities protesting the Vietnam War. Hubert Humphrey, fighting off Eugene McCarthy's anti-Vietnam crusade and inheriting Johnson's delegates, gained the nomination without having entered a single primary. Johnson's withdrawal from the '68 race only intensified the anti-war crusade at home. Meanwhile, as the body counts grew, the morass deepened in Vietnam where 58,220 U.S. soldiers, an estimated 2 million Vietnamese civilians, and an estimated 1.1 million Vietnamese and Viet Cong soldiers would ultimately perish.

The stage was set for 1969, as Boomers entered a chaotic and contentious society. Many faced difficult choices regarding military service in Vietnam, including 1.728 million draftees from 1965 to 1973, 25 percent of whom served in the war. Seventy-six percent of these were from lower/middle working-class backgrounds. Over the course of the war, the Selective Service recognized 171,000 conscientious objectors. Estimates of those who moved to Canada to escape military service vary widely, from 20,000 to 60,000 draftees. Many others (made safe by high numbers in the draft lottery) could ignore these difficult choices to pursue careers and start families. Whatever else the Vietnam War did to America and the world, it placed millions of Boomers in conflict with the demands of a U.S. war effort that half of the country viewed as a moral outrage while the U.S. government tried to sell it as the domino that would deliver all Southeast Asia to communist rule. Some felt it their duty to serve. Many had no viable alternative. Others, including me, became radicalized by what we saw as an unjust and immoral war. We were determined to resist.

And, we were aching to be born. Into our own mythos. Into our own time. After my June graduation from Hamilton, I plunked my meager savings into a BMW R60 motorcycle. I headed home to New Jersey to endure a few weeks of painful questioning (i.e. "What the hell are you doing?"). Then, with a sleeping bag, tent, and other survival items stuffed into saddlebags tied over the back seat of my two-wheeled Easy Rider, I headed west. Despite my parents' forebodings, my uncharted road trip blossomed into a journey of adventure and discovery. By the time I arrived in San Francisco three months later I had traveled 8,000 miles. It seemed like the whole country was on the road that summer. People in campers and psychedelic vans. Fellow travelers on motorcycles going nowhere in particular. You had only to flash the peace sign with your index and middle fingers, or smile and wave, for some friendly souls to stop and take you along, sharing food and fellowship and inviting you into their lives.

It still amazes me how naively trusting we were in those halcyon days. Now, fifty years later, we worry about going to a movie, a concert, a church, a synagogue or a Walmart—for fear of some crazed ideologue shooting us like fish in a barrel. Or fleeing from our homes in time to escape an oncoming hurricane, broken levee, killer flood, merciless twister, or a raging firestorm that leaps across highways and outruns cars and turns them into molten metal caskets. Today the self-aggrandizing soul that stirs spite among those fearful of the dispossessed while denying the actuality of climate change and its cataclysmic consequences is the president of the United States, Donald J. Trump, born June 14, 1946, a Boomer, proudly waving the flag he despoils as he leads us toward the abyss.

What happened? To us? To our country? Where have all the flowers gone? We, who are now older, sometimes remember simply to forget.

I digress. It was still 1968, and my 1969 adventure was yet to begin. Before graduating from college, I had applied to become a VISTA (Volunteers in Service to America) Volunteer (VV). This was the U.S. domestic Peace Corps, founded by LBJ in 1965 as part of his anti-poverty program. My acceptance would allow me, for a time, to avoid the draft and at the same time do something interesting and "worthwhile" (i.e., something I could write home about). My post-graduation sojourn would end with orders from the government to report somewhere, but I did not know when. I hoped it wouldn't be anytime soon.

I arrived in San Francisco in early September, sensing that a new me had begun to germinate from my Kerouacian summer, each day a new revelation. To survive, I moved into a residence club on Sacramento Street, an enclave of young people, mostly female, sharing apartments and dining together to live a life they could afford in the world's most beautiful city. My "apartment" was in the basement in a room consisting of two bunk beds, four guys, and a bathroom down the hall. We were "staff," paying for our Spartan existence by waiting on tables and cleaning up after the two daily meals included with the rent. I soon became smitten with a resident on the fifth floor. Sharing four roommates between us, privacy was an uncertain commodity. With 15 floors accessible by elevator, our building featured a "stairway to the stars." The door was unlocked. Along with my sky-blue tent from my summer sojourn, we dragged a mattress from a basement storage room to the roof, pitching the tent above it. Relishing our spectacular view of night-time San Francisco, we camped there for three weeks until our unsanctioned accommodations were revealed to our building manager by a tenant residing on the 16th floor of a neighboring high-rise. Paradise lost!

Soon I received orders to report to Denver. In no mood to leave the City by the Bay, I requested an alternate assignment. This afforded me three extra months in San Francisco, watching my savings dwindle but with a roof over my head and two free meals a day. December brought new orders. New Orleans. A place where I'd never been but had always wanted to go. I was to report to Austin, Texas, for training on February 19, 1969.

The Big Easy. A city of fabulous wealth, with fabled mansions on St. Charles Avenue, built early in the 20th century reflecting the opulence of its landed gentry. A city of dire poverty, with families squeezed into neighborhoods of shotgun houses where a bullet fired through the front door would go out the back door without ever hitting a wall or missing a room. White people were 50 percent of the population, I learned in my training sessions in Austin, and they lived on 80 percent of the land. Black folks, the other 50 percent, occupied the remaining 20 percent.

Was this the problem we were called upon to resolve? I pondered the hopelessness of it all. "Some things," a future New Orleans friend would tell me, "you jes caint fix."

The target areas for our anti-poverty mission were located in distinct black neighborhoods situated within or adjacent to the whiter and wealthier Uptown and Carrollton neighborhoods. Among these were Gert Town, Hollygrove, Pension Town (aka Pigeon Town) and, yes, "Nigger Town" (so-called by blacks and whites), also known as Black Pearl. With another VV, I rented a house in the center of Gert Town. The local sages told me that Gert Town was named after a famous local prostitute in the 18th century. Wikipedia differs on this, saying that it was probably named after shop owner Albert Gerhke who opened his general store there in 1893 that became a popular local hangout, partly because it hosted the area's only telephone.

Being the only white faces in an all-black neighborhood, we quickly became objects of curiosity. For me, it was like parachuting into a small African village with only a cursory familiarity with the dialect. What surprised me most was how easily we were accepted into this seemingly alien community. By volunteering in the afternoons at the local elementary school, I met many moms, most living on welfare with multiple kids in tow. I became popular with the under-ten set by giving them rides on the back of my motorcycle over the abandoned Gert Town railroad tracks, taking them airborne for a couple of exhilarating seconds. I became a regular at the Broadway Eatery, run by Miss Margaret, a large, robust, joyful black woman with unapologetic Negroid features who would burst into song whenever the spirit moved her, belting out old-time spirituals as she served up red beans, rice, sausages, fried chicken, or spaghetti with two huge meatballs for one of the premier dining experiences in "The City That Care Forgot." Picture gospel legend Mahalia Jackson (born in the Black Pearl neighborhood in 1911) singing to you as she served you lunch. It was like that. I still recall the prices. Fifty-three cents bought you the spaghetti and meatballs, and 89 cents covered two large sausages on top of a heaping pile of red beans and rice. Twelve cents more bought a refreshingly cold can of Barq's soda. The Joy Tavern just down the street became a regular hangout. When you walked in on a Saturday afternoon, it seemed that everyone in town was there, from mamas with babes in arms to elders dancing with their canes to the beat of the music. That I could walk into this scene and feel part of this welcoming community amazed me. I was blending in. "Yas'm," I would respond when Miss Margaret offered to refill my coffee. When two of my teen friends Shine and Moonie started calling me "Nigger," I understood this was the highest compliment they could bestow. "I ain't lyin'," I would respond when one of them would doubt me.

    I began to get a clue about what was happening to me on the weekly excursions of a busload of nine-year-old black boys I led every Wednesday morning from Gert Town to the magnificent indoor swimming pool of the Archdiocese of New Orleans on St. Charles Avenue. A group of white boys, same age, followed our half hour in the pool each week. These boys would march

1969: Are You Still Listening?

in silently, military style, line up along the long side of the pool, and, on command and in unison, turn right to face the pool, then, at the sound of a whistle, dive in and swim to the other side. Then, after everyone had exited the pool, they would "free swim" (do laps) for the remainder of their time. When their time elapsed, they would exit the pool, reassemble in formation, and march away.

Meanwhile, my gang of twenty or more black kids waited impatiently with pent-up excitement. I could scarcely contain them behind the swimming pool entry door. Releasing them was like unleashing a herd of feral cats into a pool of frantic mice paddling madly to save their lives.

I was beginning to love these people—these black folks. At times I found myself wishing *I* were black. Despite poverty, crime, high unemployment, and broken-down neighborhoods, so often they appeared to be living richer and more fulsome lives than my own. I was there to save *them*? I was beginning to hope they might be able to save *me*.

What to do? As a college philosophy major, the only practical skills I brought to the table were those acquired during my night-shift editorial job on the *Utica* (NY) *Daily Press* during my senior year at Hamilton. (Dad paid my college bills as I saved to buy my motorcycle.) I would start a newspaper, I decided. Hire local people to run it, to write it, to sell advertising in it. I would pull together the initial resources to publish it. I took my idea to my local mentor, Betty Wisdom, a white woman of social prominence and head of a family foundation who lived in the Carrollton neighborhood where I was working. As well, she was an activist who supported community and progressive causes, and a local sponsor of our band of neighborhood VVs. She befriended me, offering guidance as I struggled over what I might do to make a difference in the lives of these people I had volunteered to serve. She enthusiastically endorsed my idea, and promptly wrote a check for $5,000.

We were in business. We rented a storefront on Oak Street in Pension Town. With five other VVs, I moved from Gert town into a five-room shotgun on nearby Green Street. Betty suggested the name for our newspaper: *The Carrollton Advocate*. A big issue in every black neighborhood was police brutality. Police visitations could draw hundreds of people into our streets, resulting in shouting and arrests. We started to show up as well. Our randomly assigned phone number was 866-6362. After studying the possibilities of the letters assigned to these numbers, we came up with VONOFOB – Victory Over New Orleans Forces of Brutality. "When the police come into our community," we wrote, "dial VONOFOB and we will be there." "We" quickly became "me." The phone started to ring. I would get the address, get on my motorcycle, show up, and start taking pictures and asking questions. The police did not appreciate my presence. Twice thrown into jail, the film was removed from my camera on each occasion. I was released, once on the same day, the other after an unnerving overnight detention.

Soon we were publishing raw, verbatim accounts of incidents of alleged police brutality against individuals in our community. It was not long before the New Orleans power elite took notice of our activities. Jim Garrison, famed New Orleans District Attorney (1962-1973) who pursued his investigation of the Kennedy assassination, was in office at the time. Several months after *The Carrollton Advocate* began publishing, the New Orleans Police Department started its own "community newspaper." The lead in the first issue was penned by Garrison who started his message with: "Due to certain sources of misinformation that have arisen in our community, we have decided to publish..." Things grew tenser when feds sent a young man about my age, later identified as FBI informant, to enlist me in a drug deal bringing in a large marijuana shipment. I could raise $20,000 to support the newspaper, he told me. It involved a plane ride. Crazy place, New Orleans. I declined.

1969: Are You Still Listening?

From what deep resource in my white Anglo-Saxon Protestant DNA had I channeled this unfamiliar daring? Just six years earlier I was a shy, mildly rebellious teenage boy graduating from high school in a wealthy New Jersey suburb, oblivious to my future. Four years later, my only goal was to escape from the strictures of my youth and the growing monotony of life in a one-gender, largely isolated college of 800 men. Now, just one year later, I was immersed in a struggle for the rights of people who had awakened me to a world I had barely imagined, and for whom I was taking wildly unaccustomed risks. All while avoiding conscription into a foreign war that I opposed and feared in corresponding measure.

It was the sixties. Millions in my generation were discovering within them hidden springs of courage—and outrage. Yes, there were drugs involved. And music. *Political music.* Together they ignited a generational consciousness of angst and inspiration, aligning our support of civil rights with opposition to the Vietnam War into a disaffected cultural movement that our parents were no more able to understand than we were able to resist. HELL NO! We weren't going. Yes, this was war. *This was our war. We were going to win!*

The inevitable mission of every new generation is to remove blinders from the eyes of those that came before. To see the world anew. George H.W. Bush exemplified his generation's response to the massacre at Pearl Harbor and the evils of Hitler and Nazi Germany by enlisting on his 18th birthday to become the Navy's youngest fighter pilot. My uncle and namesake, Lt. Robert Langdon Coleman, born two years before Bush on December 24, 1922, was an Army fighter pilot on the Eastern Front. After his third mission, he recounted that he "lost an engine over Germany. It wasn't due to enemy action; just a case of engine failure—very rare over here. At any rate, the thing blew up and caught on fire. I got the fire out and came home on my one good engine." His final letter came from Belgium on March 27, 1945, after flying his ninth mission over Germany, escorting a Patton bomber brigade to its target. "I'll write soon," the letter ended. Four days later, his luck ran out, killed when his plane was shot down on April 1, 1945, over Gottingham, Germany.

Boomers are often compared to the Greatest Generation and found wanting. I give the Greatest Generation their due. Prevailing in WWII may be the most consequential accomplishment of any generation of Americans, past or future. George H.W. Bush was a war hero. Eisenhower. Roosevelt. Churchill. Who among us does not stand in their shadow? My uncle gave his all, perishing in a noble defense of humankind one year and one month before my birth. Did I dishonor him by taking a different path in a far different war? As part of a post-WWII generation facing conscription, we viewed the Vietnam War not simply as a peril to our survival, but as an existential, cruel and merciless threat to a country with an ancient civilization that had suffered under foreign domination for centuries past. A country that had never threatened us harm. The United States of America, our government, was prepared to bomb them back to the stone age.

We, as a generation, said "No."

Judge us as you may, this was the war that we chose, that we fought, that we won. The combined might of the federal establishment under Johnson and Nixon stepped back from the war overseas only when it became clear they were losing the war at home.

However we may be judged by the generation that preceded us and those that follow, we delivered our explicit, obstinate, and often eloquent messages about the world we were born into, and about the war we were determined to end.

And the world listened.

Elvis Presley, the *King of Rock and Roll*, meets with Richard Nixon in the Oval Office to accept an honorary Bureau of Narcotics badge.

Astronaut Buzz Aldrin, lunar module pilot, walks on the moon during Apollo 11 mission; "First Man" Neil Armstrong captures the moment.

1969: Are You Still Listening?

The Beatles' unannounced 42-minute concert on the rooftop of Apple Corps became their final public performance, January 30, 1969.

Controversies dogged Richard Nixon throughout his political career, from receiving graft as a congressman to the Watergate Scandal.

1969: Are You Still Listening?

Confronting intense pressure from anti-Vietnam War protests, Richard Nixon tries to placate and disengage American combat forces.

Operation Rolling Thunder was an aggressive bombing campaign by the U.S. military and Vietnam Air Force against North Vietnam.

The My Lai Massacre was one of the most unfathomable acts of violence committed against unarmed civilians during the Vietnam War.

At the conclusion of Woodstock, hippies became unhappy with jacked-up food prices, so a few burned down vendor stalls in protest.

CHAPTER NINE

Freedom Tastes of Reality

By Brent Green

Half of her right eyebrow curved up while the other half curved down. "Keep your eyes on him," she lectured Beauchamp. "It's going to hit him like a brick shithouse."

Esmeralda, as she declared herself, had just produced three gelatin capsules filled with amorphous brown powder. She had quickly accepted our money and stashed three Hamilton's somewhere under her granny dress. She had not mentioned a brick shithouse before concluding negotiations and a sale.

Schmidt and Beauchamp popped pills into their mouths and chased them with impressive swigs of Southern Comfort, a favored libation of the newly discovered Texas blues-rock singer Janis Joplin. It seemed fitting. Capsule still rolling indecisively on my open hand, they coaxed me to swallow it whole.

"Shouldn't I take, like, half?" I suggested.

"No, man. Do the whole thing. Otherwise, you may not get off. There's a threshold, you know."

I studied my two co-conspirators who had lured me to Esmeralda's house somewhere in the suburbs of south Houston. The house was middle class but situated in a lower-middle-class neighborhood, making her hippie haven seem palatial by contrast. The boys were thrilled to be consuming a psychedelic substance with promises of transportation to another galaxy of consciousness. It had been a long, dry summer in the most drug-adverse state anywhere. We were head-starved. Time to trip out, boys. Maybe a chance to meet God?

"I don't want to freak out. This is my first trip."

"We'll keep an eye on you," Beauchamp promised. He towered above us, all leathers, feathers, symbols, and laces. His chiseled face could have been a parody of Clint Eastwood in *Hang 'Em High*.

"Who's guiding me?" I asserted.

Schmidt shot Beauchamp an exasperated glance and spoke as if I wasn't present. "Well, hell, he can empty his capsule and swallow half now, and if he doesn't get off in an hour or two, he can do the other half."

"Groovy," said Schmidt. Looking at me, he added, "Just do it now, not later."

Orbiting on another planet, Esmeralda studied us, not happy that we had invaded her space but knowing it was necessary for her to be a disinclined drug dealer. Scoring for us required her to provide a trip-pad since we had no other convenient place to journey without encountering straight people. She needed money; we required mind expansion in her estate. Staring me down with piercing intensity, she said, "Take the whole thing if you want a good trip. It won't kill you. Go ahead, take it."

Peer pressure hit me as if running face first into a fire hose, a sense of gushing obligation. I didn't want to offend. Ever. What did I have to lose? I swallowed the capsule with a flourish and a polite "Fuck you," grabbed the Southern Comfort bottle, and chased the pill down with an impressive swig.

Esmeralda examined the other two again. "Keep an eye on him until he comes down. I'm not responsible for what happens to any of you. I'm a facilitator, not a babysitter."

"Why am I in danger and not these two?"

"You're young and innocent," she said.

"I'm the same age as Schmidt; Beauchamp is two years older."

Esmeralda lit a Marlboro cigarette and plopped down at her kitchen table. "Age doesn't have anything to do with it. These two are seasoned. I can tell by their auras."

Feeling a warm stomach buzz from Janis's favorite libation, I started giggling.

"You two are responsible for anything that happens," she said nodding my direction. "That stuff is going to crush him like a brick shithouse."

Laughing, I said, "What the hell is a brick shithouse?"

Beauchamp cleared his throat. "It's urban for a large, very well-built man—the kind of dude you never want to mess with.

"When applied to a street drug of unknown purpose, strength, and origin, it means your head may travel through a wormhole to somewhere else and not come back."

"That would suck," I said.

"Psychotic City," said Schmidt.

Schmidt, whose face was all curly beard growing too long to look groomed in a recent decade, had Socratic eyes and a habit of turning an idle conversation into philosophical discourse. "She's referring to a toilet—built from brick. Like, solid, dude. Can compress your brains—but don't worry about it."

Tingles of anxiety crept up my spine. I could visualize the capsule decomposing in my stomach to release an unknown psychoactive substance into my digestive system, the circulatory system, and eventually lighting a fire to my nervous system where havoc might happen. I deliberated vomiting.

Come on baby, light my fire. I slugged down another shot of Southern Comfort while wondering if chugging the amber liquid could be an expedient way to induce barfing. Throwing up would relieve me of pre-trip anxieties. I squared off with Schmidt and asked, "If you're supposed to look after me should I start getting weird, who's looking after you? And Beauchamp?"

"Lucy."

Schmidt and Beauchamp laughed. Esmeralda blew a smoke ring, appearing pissed.

I said, "Who's Lucy and where is the lady?"

"In the sky with diamonds," said Schmidt.

"You'll know it's her when you come upon a girl with the sun in her eyes," Beauchamp added.

My drug-tripping antagonists sniggered, confirming that Esmeralda's product had kicked into second gear.

"Okay. I can be the butt of your jokes, but I don't need two jerkoffs dissecting my psyche."

Schmidt became serious. "Just messing with you, Buddy, to help you relax."

"So you'll enjoy the trip," added Beauchamp.

Sensing a subtle shift from first to second gear, I had grown weary of innuendos, their implied sense of drug-guiding superiority. "You know what? I'm going to split and leave the three of you to amuse each other."

Alarm covered Beauchamp's face. "NO! You can't split. You can't drive. You must stay here where we can guide your trip."

"Piss on your guided adventure. This is not fun. Besides, Schmidt, your face looks like a fat furry squirrel." I sauntered to the kitchen door leading to a driveway, opened it, and stepped outside. A fog of hot, humid air fell over me.

Schmidt rushed to grab my arm. "You're safe. We'll take care of you. That's what buddies are for."

"No thanks. I'm splitting."

Beauchamp stepped outside behind Schmidt. "He's right—this is the safest place in the world for you to travel beyond the doors of perception."

Schmidt pulled his beard with a Socratic flourish, his eyes becoming unfocused, and he launched into a monologue. "You will be traveling through another dimension, a dimension not only of sight and sound but of mind. A journey into a wondrous land of imagination...

"Next stop, the Twilight Zone!" announced Beauchamp and Schmidt in unison. They laughed and tugged my arm to pull me back into the kitchen and Esmeralda's dominion. I obeyed, zoned-out, zombielike.

Wall-papered with poppy-like floral patterns, her garish kitchen had become electronic with colors melting into each other. I noticed the loamy fragrance of a cat litter next to her stove and then recalled Grandma Jessie's kitchen on a farm near Norton, Kansas, where organic odors created a daily narrative of life meeting death meeting life. Once she chopped off the head of a chicken as a prelude to Sunday dinner, and the decapitated creature ran in wide circles around her front yard for five minutes. I declined a Southern-fried drumstick several hours later and opted instead for homegrown corn-on-the-cob. These memories made me nauseous and ravenous all at once.

"Brick shithouse," Esmeralda announced.

Schmidt shepherded me into her living room, which had been decorated as if an oil painting created by Salvador Dali. A novelty clock melted off the edge of a coffee table. An intricate and bejeweled praying mantis statuette graced an end table. Old-fashioned crutches, hand-carved entirely of oak, leaned against the front door, announcing that nobody should enter or exit there. A large lobster pillow defended her divan. Cellophane flowers of yellow and green burst from a cobalt blue vase. All these things became fluid, interacting with one another, animated and living.

Esmeralda's lifestyle may have been Spartan, but she valued music and had spent a bundle on a bodacious Harman Kardon stereo system. Spinning on her Gerrard turntable, Sgt. Pepper's band overwhelmed the house with parading music.

Picture yourself in a boat on a river

With tangerine trees and marmalade skies

Somebody calls you, you answer quite slowly

A girl with kaleidoscope eyes

Lucy again, that Lucy, guiding our trips through the exigencies of being. The rush of it all, the temporality of everything. All the choices to make and not make: freedom to some, the weightiness of being to others.

It occurred to me that Beauchamp and Schmidt were victims. I couldn't quite coalesce the cobwebs of my mind into a coherent construct then, but I could see that the world around us commanded risk-taking with imprudent pharmaceutical exploration. Reality sucked in 1969, even with NASA's Apollo, monumental and moon-bound. Jungle war. Death. Uptightness everywhere. Prejudices abounding. Stereotyping. Conformity. Lost souls, lost generation. Youth suppressed and depressed. Nowhere to go but inward. Then outward in bellicose lockstep marches against authority. Assassinations. Corporate plutocracy. Strangling Mother Nature to death. One hell of a way to become 19, living inside the nightmares and paranoias of Richard Nixon and Spiro Agnew.

Patterns formed and dissolved into each other as Esmeralda's capsules insisted that reality is inside the mind, a universe of possibilities. Inside, liberation from "the way God meant us to be."

Granny dress shimmering, Esmeralda drifted into her living room looking suspicious and tentative. "Keep your eyes on him," she instructed.

For the next period, I could no longer measure movement forward from the formation of the earth. I obsessed over her Daliesque crazy clock to put a framework around ordinary consciousness. Clock hands moved counterclockwise. I climbed into the back of my head where all perceptions became clouds lacking form or substance, a misty world detached from analysis or judgment. Ego-dissolution says the scientists. A place where light became white and nothing else.

Esmeralda stared at me, still; I could feel her eyes upon me. Beauchamp and Schmidt turned away, lost inside the back of their heads. But, as if we had become astral projections of ourselves, we connected through conscious awareness and communication that didn't need to be spoken. They were taking care of me, and Lucy was taking care of them taking care of me. And it was Esmeralda's fault. Everything clarified itself.

A large, gray cat jumped onto the coffee table, purring. It grinned. "What do you call this?"

"Chess," said Esmeralda.

I studied the animal as it scoped me out. "It smiles."

"It knows a revolution is in the air," she said.

"Her? Him?"

"Both—IT," she insisted.

As if a dream coming gradually into focus, only Chess's grin remained in my swirling imagination, a hallucination emitting bursts of energy, giving way to skewed patterns of cognition, imagination, and ambitious fantasies.

"It teaches us the rules," she announced to a sonorous room. The disembodied cat smile vibrated in and out of existence, and I became lost in the journey, ethereal as Chess.

An hour later, maybe ten, Schmidt interrupted the Pinball Wizard, a psychosomatic deaf, dumb, and blind boy, to ask an obvious question, the query that should have been issued before we ventured into pharma hinterland.

"Tommy, can you hear me?" he asked nobody.

"Can you feel me near you?" said Beauchamp in rejoinder.

Schmidt stood from his lotus pose and seemed angry. His eyes boring holes into Esmeralda, he asked, "What is that shit you sold us?"

"A ticket to ride," she answered with matter-of-fact clarity.

"We need to know. What is that shit? Your brick shithouse?"

"Chocolate acid."

If someone can truly look blown away, Schmidt appeared blown with hurricane force. "Chocolate acid!"

"That's the stuff God warned us about," said Beauchamp. "LSD laced with speed. It can ruin your teeth from grinding."

"It can ruin your skull from schizophrenia," lamented Schmidt. "My head has circled Saturn twice. I had to hold my brain in both hands to keep it from flying away on a 747."

"I've carried the weight of this brick shithouse long enough," I insisted. "I'm going home. I've seen enough insanity for this lifetime."

Nodding agreement, Schmidt said to Esmeralda, "Don't expect to see us again. You sold us one thing and delivered another."

"The walls come tumbling, tumbling down," she said.

"Do we give a shit, guys?" said Beauchamp as reconciliation.

"This shithouse has changed everything," I said. "I cannot see anything the same way again. You are part of this for as long as I contain memories."

"Fifty years?" Schmidt teased.

"Twenty-nineteen and beyond."

"That's a heavy burden to carry for so many decades. Lots of bricks on your shoulders, man."

"Shit, too," I reminded.

I studied two quasi-brothers—well-meaning but manipulative—who had become adversaries and then friends again. I understood them as living enigmas, another couple of long-hair freaks trying to sort through insanities of a world they had not created. A world of war, injustice, street riots, poverty, dead rivers and lakes, subjugation, which included everyone plus white male Anglo-Saxon Protestants. Like us. They were bad boys and innocent children all at once. The targets of repression. "You're forgiven for the brick shithouse crushing my boyish soul. I understand now what it's all about."

"What's it all about?" asked Schmidt.

"I'm free. And freedom tastes of reality." I turned to leave through the front door, which had been blocked with Dali's crutches. I pushed them out of the way as Esmeralda screamed her protest. "I'm expecting you to follow me!"

"Freaks!" I stepped outside and slammed the door, traveling away from that part of my life, never to return to uncharted psychological chaos that psychedelic drugs can portend. Beauchamp became a famous Houston DJ who landed an hour-long interview with Bruce Springsteen just before The E Street Band and The Boss became rock gods. He died in the mid-1980s for reasons not clarified on the internet. Schmidt could be anywhere or dead. Esmerelda too.

CHAPTER TEN

Of Miniskirts, Misdeeds, and Moon Missions

By Greg Dobbs

Sure, there were world-changing moments in 1969—the counter-culture of Woodstock, the debut of Boeing's gigantic 747, the inauguration of Richard Nixon, the first human steps on the moon.

But looking back, 1969 for me is not so meaningful because of what we as a generation saw, or did, or thought, or felt, or learned.

No, it is meaningful for me on a much more personal level: 1969 is when I got my first full-time, career-centric, grown-up job in journalism. And reflecting on how we did our work back then, looking back to 1969 is looking back to how we've changed. As Elizabeth Barrett Browning once wrote, "Let me count the ways."

I'll give you but a few.

It was in late '69 that I got a job producing the newscasts of the already legendary biggest voice on radio, Paul Harvey. If you're old enough, you'll remember Paul's signature lead-ins to commercials in his unparalleled oral blend of baritone and bass: "Page TWO!" And his signature sign-off: "Paul Harvey. Good DAY."

It was his concise use of the language, and the stylistically dramatic breaks in his delivery, that helped make Paul so popular. I used to joke that I wrote all Paul's pauses (there was a good three or four-second gap in that sign-off, between "Paul Harvey" and "Good DAY"). But besides imparting news items both essential and eclectic, Paul Harvey was a commentator. That's why the show was titled, *Paul Harvey News and Comment*.

And that's why looking back on 1969 is instructive today. Because Paul Harvey was a gentleman. His politics weren't my politics—he was a solid conservative (although the label back then carried a different meaning than it does these days). But never uncivil, never strident, never insulting, never harsh.

Could you say that about commentators on the air today? The Rush Limbaughs, the Ann Coulters, the Sean Hannitys? Maybe even Stephen Colbert deserves a place on the list.

1969 is instructive because it taught me to believe you can coat your comments with sugar and still make your point.

Paul did. He was never bitter. And, in contrast to the voices out there today, never myopic. I remember one day when he delivered his script to my desk; since ABC Radio News broadcast his newscasts, I was the company's filter, and he was obliged to run everything past me. Well, Paul that morning had been leafing through the wire services we had in the office—AP, UPI, Reuters—and had seen some unrelated statistics in two separate stories. One was about miniskirts; they were getting shorter. The other was about crime; the rate of rapes was going up. Paul put two and two together and came up with five, writing in that day's commentary that shorter skirts were spurring on more American men to commit rape.

1969: Are You Still Listening?

Having perhaps a more modern impression than he did about what motivates rapists, I told Paul that I thought he had cooked up a careless conclusion. And that's all it took. He killed the piece.

With the ideologically rigid commentators out there today, can you even imagine that happening? Either they wall themselves off and, like too many Americans today in all walks of life, only read and listen to information that fits their narrative—or even worse, they know something's fictitious, but it fits their fan base, so they put it out there anyway.

I learned about integrity in journalism from Paul Harvey way back in 1969. But today? Mindful of how Brent Green ends this book's introduction, "Let the past remind us of what we are not now," I am still listening, and I don't like what I hear.

In May 1969, before going to work with Harvey, I got a five-month job as a temporary field producer for ABC Television News. It was called a "summer replacement" position, to fill in for full-time producers taking their vacations. I was barely qualified, but the news business was still in an era of full employment and having been an intern in a San Francisco newsroom while attending the University of California at Berkeley, I was the best they could get for a job that was scheduled to expire.

What a lucky break—especially since, after finishing my two-and-a-half years with Paul Harvey, it led to a job as a full-time producer for ABC News, and a few years later, two decades as a correspondent, with assignments all over the nation and all around the world, none of which I would trade. In '69 of course, fresh out of grad school, I couldn't see any of that coming. It opened the door to undertakings in that Summer of '69 like a very special trip to a town called Wapakoneta, Ohio.

That might not strike you as special until you learn, Wapakoneta was the hometown of Neil Armstrong, the first human to step on the moon. On July 20, 1969, we would broadcast live from Wapakoneta, and I got to help produce the program. If people clear across this planet were excited about America's moon landing that day, no nation was more excited than ours, and within the United States, no community was more excited than Wapakoneta.

Sad to say though, looking back fifty years later, that day in 1969 probably was both the first and the last time we all came together, citizens on every continent struck with a single sense of awe. Today, between irreparable gaps in people's opportunities and irreconcilable forms of religious extremism, great advances in technology can be as easily abused and sometimes condemned as they are appreciated.

In the latter years of my television career, NASA came back into play. I had become an anchor and senior correspondent (along with Dan Rather) for an all-high-definition television network called HDNet (which since has morphed into AXS TV). And when NASA asked HDNet for some technical help documenting every detail of every space shuttle launch after the catastrophe with shuttle Columbia, the network's founder Mark Cuban said yes, and decided to take it up a step and do a live broadcast for our audience from the Kennedy Space Center of every subsequent launch. I was tapped to anchor those hour-and-a-half shows.

We broadcast about 35 more flights from Florida before the shuttle program ended, and I wouldn't trade a single one. Every launch was somehow unique: a different time of day or night, a different sky in the background, a different threat from the weather, a different malfunction from the ship's two million parts, a different crew in the orbiter, a different trajectory, sometimes a different mission. I was struck every time—and frankly, I hope this came across on the air—with a sense of admiration for the audacity of the astronauts, a sense of awe for the brainpower of the engineers and scientists behind them, and a sense of patriotism that it was my country, my people, who were shooting for the stars. Man was meant to explore; America was the unrivaled pioneer in the cosmos.

1969: Are You Still Listening?

But how much did the public care? After the first exceptional achievements in space, not so much. The head of one of the biggest private corporations in the space business told me during one broadcast from Florida that he was having trouble attracting bright minds to work in the space sector. It wasn't exciting anymore. It was old news.

And today's attitude? Space is too costly. Space is too competitive. Our leaders talk more about space as a platform for weapons than as a platform for exploration.

"Let the past remind us of what we are not now?" Some days, I'd rather not be reminded.

Finally, 1969 was the beginning of the Nixon era. I never laid eyes on the man until he was re-nominated in 1972 when I was producer-in-charge of ABC's mobile unit (a huge semi-truck with live cameras the size of telephone booths) at that summer's two political party conventions, which were both in Miami. But if you'll permit a bit of a stretch (he did begin his presidency in '69), I'll tell you how it seems, looking back.

It seems that little has changed. Once Nixon got into trouble over Watergate, he blamed (among others) the media. Sound familiar? In those days, television news crews still recorded stories on film, using those big black cameras with what we called "Mickey Mouse" ears on top, which housed the reels of 16mm film. That made us visible every time we got on an airplane.

And Nixon supporters who spotted us, angry at the media because they were following the president's lead, would accuse us in so many words, "You people are out to make Nixon look like a crook." To which I would typically respond, "Sir (or ma'am), we can't make anyone look like a crook—or a liar, or a cheater, or a fool without his help."

I find myself saying it again today.

It's not that we don't have a better world now than we had fifty years ago. In many ways, probably most ways, we do. A fellow journalist a long time ago wrote an illuminating book with an equally illuminating title: *The Good Old Days...They Were Terrible*. In countless ways, they were.

But while our world has gotten better since 1969, it's only better by some measures. We sometimes are less civil than we were, we sometimes use technology to do harm instead of good, and we sometimes are blind to those who corrupt our politics.

In the 1800s, French journalist Jean-Baptiste Alphonse Karr wrote, "The more things change, the more they stay the same." Fifty years since 1969, he could write the same thing. Sometimes we haven't been listening.

CHAPTER ELEVEN

I Pledge Allegiance

By Brent Green

My eyes snapped open to see a misty apparition—a hooded face, black and featureless. I had been sleeping in the same bunk every night for six months, so I knew the dorm belonged to reality. The face staring at me, however, was a spook from another century. As waking reality formed shape and substance, I saw more clearly a face covered by a cloth with two holes for eyes and a triangle for nostrils. A dark hood covered its head, and it moved nearer to my face, roughly commanding, "Get up." The Ku Klux Klan?

I pushed up on my elbows and surveyed the dorm. Bunks full of slumbering bodies lined the long room, but nobody else stirred to witness this phantasmagoria. I didn't know whether to lash out or run. Instead, I climbed down, stepping carefully on the lower bunk to avoid Irving Robert's fat legs, and a frigid cement floor shot up my spine.

Wrapping my arms around myself and tiptoeing to the door, I glanced around and shivered—more from a sudden rush of aloneness than frozen floors. A robed arm, index finger extended, pointed my path. I knew the direction, but I didn't know where I was going, feeling as if this might be my first moments in hell.

The familiar hallway had been dimly lit with rows of candle jars spraying orange light across the walls, and my practiced late-night passage to the bathroom had become a cave orifice. Halfway to the john, another robed figure stood, beckoning me forward. Glancing left and right at lightless study rooms on either side, I wondered if something wicked would pounce from one of those black doorways as I passed. I glanced over my shoulder at the waker, standing erect and solid. He angrily motioned me to move down the hallway. Monotonous, distant chanting demanded that I struggle forward.

After days of sleeplessness, my foggy mind had difficulty distinguishing fact and fiction. I knew I was awake, but I pinched my naked leg to make sure. My feet shuffled toward the next monk. A brown robe, reaching to his ankles, had been tied at the waist with a braided gold rope. A hood surrounded his head, and his face was covered with black material. He pointed toward a bathroom door. Chanting volume increased. I hesitated, and he jerked his arm up as if to hit me and pointed brusquely again at the closed door. I stood dumbly still, resisting the command to move into the bathroom. His hood pushed into my face, and his arms flailed in exaggeration as if a scarecrow and I pushed through the door.

The bathroom had been lit like the hallway, candles everywhere. Windows had been covered with cardboard and taped shut. Three-foot-high stereo speakers sat on chairs at either end of the room, and Tibetan chants blared. The room was otherwise empty.

I investigated a mirror above a row of sinks to see myself in dull, ocher light. I looked as I always appeared in the middle of the night: hair chaotic, eyes puffy, a resemblance of me—but not quite—more of a haggard, harried me. A shadow outlined my beard. The bathroom floor felt dry and warm to my bare feet.

Investigating the community shower, I found more candles on a dry floor. The bathroom door flew open and Sam Walken, my roommate, stumbled into the makeshift penitentiary. Dressed only in boxer shorts, he seemed equally disoriented, and I walked over to reassure him.

A monk opened the swinging door and motioned with his index finger for us not to speak. Then another man stumbled through the door, then another, and another, and another.

Within twenty-five minutes the bathroom filled with all twenty-four of us. A towering monk walked into the bathroom and clapped his hands loudly at several whisperers. They shut up. The monk pulled a handful of papers from underneath his robe and distributed one page to each of us.

It was an oath—a long oath, verbose and archaic. At the bottom of the page were instructions: memorize the oath word-for-word without speaking. We would be severely tested in front of a Grand Tribunal.

Soon the warm room reeked of body odor. Some sat on johns, lids down; others sat on the shower floor. I found solitude under a sink and began to repeat the oath to myself, again and again. I studied and rehearsed and watched others as they watched me. We'd exchange grins or exaggerated sighs, but this had become serious business, and the heaviness of perfect recollection felt intense. Between us and fraternal initiation stood this oath, and we had to get it right. I said it over and over until I could recite it flawlessly. Then the chanting stopped.

I heard voiceless sounds: feet shuffling, lips clapping, a cough or cleared throat. But soon Ravel's *Boléro* blasted into the dank bathroom, stereo volume way too loud, forcing us to wince. The music delivered a refreshing change from monotonous chants, but as the record played and replayed, I began to detest its mechanistic insistence.

Every ten minutes a monk appeared at the door and beckoned one of us. Danny Williams left the room, and I imagined him walking guiltily toward a rigid firing squad. They blindfolded him and shouted, "Ready, aim—FIRE!", then Danny folded onto himself, an empty sack.

As if reciting the Pledge of Allegiance, words spilled off my silent tongue until I tripped. The ancient oath had been filled with frilly words that lent no added meaning, and I always failed with one of the unnecessary adjectives or adverbs. A self-conscious person must have written this oath when filigree was as popular in language as in art. The words pretended something profound, but one had to dig away too many weeds and worms to find anything of literary merit. I rehearsed until the oath became meaningless.

With time, anxiety filled the hot room. Candles flickered, and shadows danced across the walls, adding dizzying movement to the spell. We had no concept of night or day.

Eventually half of us remained. I had been the first to be awakened. Why had I not been first to go before the Tribunal? Anger seethed through me: I thought about slamming open that prison door and escaping wretched absurdity.

Then they beckoned my roommate. I sent him a sympathetic message with my eyebrows. Acknowledging me with a nod, he hung his head and walked into the hall. His obsequious exit buttressed my rage. Who are these clansmen that they treat us with such dishonor?

I staggered into a stall and heaved dry gasps into the stool, but I didn't puke because my stomach had been emptied for hours. I couldn't eat the lousy stew they had forced upon us as supper. It had been full of matchbooks, dog food, chili peppers, cigarette butts, dead cockroaches, and condoms, the question of whether used or not still lingering. Thoughts of "happy stew" caused me to heave again.

The bathroom door swung open once more, and the messenger pointed at me. I unrolled some toilet paper and wiped sputum from my chin, stood and faced him squarely. This was a fucking game—a child's concept of malicious fun. They would not make this important to me; they could only require me to go through the motions. I didn't hang my head but walked severely into a cool breeze and dark hallway.

The escort motioned me toward a stairwell leading down three flights to a chapter meeting room. Lights had been turned off, so stairs fell into an inky cavern. Silver light from a setting moon spilled through a solitary picture window, lending some reassurance upon my witnessing this cold January orb. At the bottom of the stairs, yellow candlelight filtered through a doorway. I hesitated at the final step, but my escort pushed me toward the threshold, and I moved tentatively into a large recreation room. A lustrous and immaculate floor reflected all the hours it had taken my pledge brothers to clean, strip, wax, and buff dilapidated linoleum.

I rounded a corner to face a semi-circle of monks swaying silently in candlelight. Behind them, hooded shadows nodded with eerie syncopation on concrete walls. In the center of their semi-circle, a brass lamp had been left on a Bible that, in turn, lay on a waist-high wood table. My escort fell away into a midnight background. Their ornate oath swirled through my head in meaningless fragments. I could not then even recall the first sentence.

Self-consciously, I squinted to read exposed pages from the Book, searching for significance and hidden meaning. The Bible had been opened to the Book of Job, but I could not read the chaotic type. Small and brassy, the lamp looked like the historical lamp of learning; a single wick burned with orange and blue flame; and the area smelled of pungent, burning oil. A polished brass finish reflected my white T-shirt and distorted head. Still, nobody spoke.

In the absence of instructions, I guessed that my test was to recite the oath spontaneously, so I cleared my throat and opened my mouth to speak. One monk lurched toward me as if Dr. Frankenstein's monster dragging a useless leg. He grasped the lamp and held it before my face.

My mind raced. I calculated that the lamp symbolized learning. To accept the lamp must mean that I would willingly accept the challenges of my college education. But his intimidating presentation also made me suspicious. A trick?

The monk waited as I weighed my decision, the flame burning close to my eyes, and I could see nothing else but his anonymous onyx face behind a hood. So, I accepted the lamp. Nothing moved, nobody spoke. Seconds passed. Some gasps. The swaying Tribunal became motionless. Someone switched on severe overhead florescent bulbs, and the room became flooded with sterile white light. I squinted with pain.

The lead Tribunal monk ripped off his hood and mask: Dan Bouchard, the "High Rho" or ritualist. "You kept the lamp!" Bochard narrowed his eyes and said, "You stupid shit—how could you be so dumb? Haven't you learned anything?"

Blood rushed to my face. "But—isn't it the lamp of learning? I thought you gave me the lamp of learning!"

Another chapter active tore off his facemask. Jerry Smith said, "Get him out of here. He's ruined our perfect record!"

Gary Lockhead roughly grabbed my arm and escorted me toward the stairwell. I heard people shouting at each other and cursing my name.

Lockhead, Joe Finch and Fred Winter pushed me up the stairs, and my legs became stiff and clumsy. They said nothing. We reached my room, and Lockhead pushed me into a chair next to my desk. Towering above me, Joe Finch butchered me with his dark, fiery gaze.

"You kept the lamp!" Finch said. "I thought you were smart. How could you be so stupid?"

The room felt frigid, adding to my sense of isolation. "I don't understand. I didn't know—"

"You get it? You kept the lamp," scolded Gary Lockhead, my pledge father. "You didn't think for a second about your brothers, did you?"

I was astonished because Gary had been my ally throughout the fall semester. He had helped me adjust to fraternity life, had counseled me about studying, and had introduced me to a few sorority women. The easygoing senior had never said a harsh word to me.

I said, "I didn't understand. What should I have done?"

Gary answered, "You should have taken the lamp, but immediately you must give it back. The lamp represents brotherhood. You share a bond; you don't keep it to yourself." He brushed past me and left the room.

Chapter president Fred Winter leveled an angry gaze at me. I had always admired his maturity and sound judgment. "Do you know what this means? Alumni could shut down the house for our failure to train you properly! What you did was worse than I can imagine—you kept the lamp!" He looked at Finch and said, "Take him back to the meeting room. He owes our entire chapter an apology."

"I'll say anything."

Finch said, "Nothing you can say or do will erase this failure. You are a disgrace. I hope some seniors don't tear you a new asshole. On second thought—I'll help them!"

Goose pimples covered my arms and legs. "I'll move out now."

"You'll be lucky to get your stuff packed," Winter said. He looked back at Finch and added, "As much as I hate to protect his ass, we better assign guards. His pledge brothers are likely to beat the crap out of him."

Finch shrugged, "Whatever. You're the boss. But I vote against bodyguards."

"I am the boss," Fred Winter said. "Get two other guys and cover this stupid plebe. Despite what we feel, we must protect him. The Inter-Fraternity Council expects it. Can you imagine what other fraternities will say when they hear about this?" He also stalked out of the room.

Feeling nauseous, I saw my reputation and future flushing down the toilet as dry, ineffectual heaves. I could still detect distant moaning of *Boléro*.

"I'm dropping out," I said.

"Like a pussy quitter," Finch spit.

Nobody would screw with Finch: he was a badass brute from North Kansas City. He specialized in looking mean. Pledges had become universally fearful of his wrath. I was at least twenty-five pounds lighter, four or five inches shorter and a lot less athletically toned. He had all the earmarks of the most loutish bully anyone might remember from high school. But a couple of years before, I had been a gymnast, my specialty the pommel horse. My forearms were taut, and my triceps ripped. But I was in my skivvies, broken down from many sleepless nights, worked over, and resentful beyond common sense. I tried to block my raging fantasies.

Then Finch made a mistake of roughly grabbing my arm to jerk me to my feet. Holding me firmly and saying nothing more, he thrust me toward the door. I was tight and could not breathe. I looked over my shoulder and squinted at his snarling smile, instantly saw his sadistic pleasure, and with all my remaining strength, I spun around and belted him square on the nose—not once, but twice: two quick, dead-on pops.

Before his hands could reach his nose, blood started spewing from both nostrils. I began to move left and right to avoid his groping arms. He made another mistake of lunging at me. I had no intention of going down, and despite the vast differences in our size and weight, I knew I wouldn't. While I felt fearful, I also embraced exhilaration; I had not felt this much power for months. He tried to hit me back, but I scored with my left jab, spreading blood over his mouth and chin. I must have hit him with a dozen more left jabs, and then a solid right to his solar plexus. He nailed me back with a lucky right, barely bruising my cheek. I staggered him again with a loaded left hook, and he shouted at the top of his lungs for help. I was beyond control,

1969: Are You Still Listening?

seething with a vengeance after many months of humiliation and subjugation.

Winter and three other robed men ran into my room and grabbed me. I struggled to breathe and free myself of them, but they shouted for me to cool down—everything was going to be all right they said; this was part of the ritual. I realized I had a terrible headache, and finally, I went limp, threatening all of them not to fuck with me again or they would have to haul my ass out of there in an ambulance before I would stop retaliating.

Winter said, "Somebody escort Finch to the emergency room." Looking at me, he spoke gently, "We let this get too far out of hand. We pushed you to the edge, and you went over. We should have known better than to let Finch be your interrogator."

I told him I was ready to start packing. I wasn't about to apologize to anyone for nailing that asshole Finch. He'd been hazing my butt since the first week of the semester.

Winter said to the others, "Take him back to the initiation room for reconciliation. We'll deal with this outburst later. And, for God's sake, get somebody to clean up this blood."

They gently nudged me toward the stairwell, and I staggered, numb. I glimpsed outside through the stairwell window again and noticed dawn breaking above the horizon. I noticed lights in the windows of a nearby fraternity house, and I wished I had never pledged in the first place. My body, a zombie, followed.

The Tribunal had returned to formation. Overhead lights had been turned off, and the room was aglow with candlelight. In front of the lamp of learning, two other pledges waited. I wanted to run, to pull away. I expected harsh stares of recrimination, but they hung their heads and did not look at me. One sobbed. I thought he must be stricken with my failure and angry outburst; lack of acknowledgment as I approached stung more than condemnation. My body sagged with weight.

The Tribunal swayed in syncopation. One of the monks spoke softly, quoting from the scriptures. He talked about Jesus, human frailty, sin, and forgiveness.

We were being forgiven. My pledge brothers and I had committed the same contrived sin. It did not matter whether we had kept the lamp or given it back; either way, we would have failed the test and been pushed away into contrived sessions of interrogation and mortification. The ritual had been designed to make us understand failure, forgiveness and—brotherhood. We were being taught a Biblical lesson of human imperfection and the virtue of compassion followed by absolution.

My relief commingled with a bitter taste. We had been manipulated, but joy rushed into me. I thought about Vietnam concentration camps: my will had almost been broken as if I had been a prisoner of war. I could not erase from my mind's eye Finch's sneer—his brutal grin. For him, this hadn't been just an initiation ritual. Free of failure's harrowing burdens I suddenly felt exhilarated—done with it at last.

For a few months, my search for meaning ended inside a small book of secret rituals. Their values became my values. Even as I stood shivering before the Tribunal during the final moments of forgiveness, I wanted to administer the same ritual to another group of naïve pledges. I wanted to become their judgment day. Mind control can be magic.

But I couldn't shake hypocrisy. Finch's nose mended, but I never spoke to him again in private. We avoided each other at public functions. Although the ritual had been embellished with Christian symbolism, it mocked the brotherly love that Finch had desecrated.

In the end, those final days of my fraternity months in college had exacted too large a toll for forgiveness. It had cost me innocence. And from that misty, lingering, chanting, sonic, smelly, blood-smeared night forward, it has been difficult for me to pledge allegiance to most authorities. This seems to be true for my generation, at large.

Tailpiece

Fraternities and sororities on college campuses experienced a healthy membership resurgence following years of decline during the Great Depression and World War II. But during the late 1960s, widespread political, social, and cultural upheaval threatened the Greek system. In reaction to a widely unpopular Vietnam War and the military draft, social and political justice causes exploded at a dizzying pace on the nation's campuses to include rejection of many forms of authority or tradition. Starting on the east and west coasts and then migrating to major urban areas, it soon became unpopular to become or remain a fraternity or sorority member. To many college students of that time, being Greek became antithetical to being iconoclastic and revolutionary in spirit, inconsistent with emerging value consensus. The numbers of pledges and sustaining actives dropped dramatically. A milieu of protest spared no organized campus group, and Greek chapter after chapter closed. The Greek system has never fully recovered from the late 60s and 70s.

Even now, fifty years since the Greek system began a downhill slide, fraternities and sororities occasionally become the focus of intense media and public criticism because of ongoing problems with elitism, alcohol abuse, hazing, sexism, and sometimes rape cultures.

CHAPTER TWELVE

The Promise

By Jed Diamond, Ph.D.

On a dark November night in 1969, my life changed forever. But for my story to make sense, I need to go back twenty years to the summer of 1949. I was five years old that year when my uncle drove me to a mental hospital. I was confused and afraid.

"Why do I have to go?" I asked Uncle Harry.

He looked at me with his round face and kind eyes. "Your father needs you."

"What's the matter with him?" I was beginning to cry, and I clamped my throat tight to stop the tears.

He turned away and looked back at the road. In our family, we didn't talk about difficult issues. I knew that my father was in a hospital and it was my duty to visit him. It never occurred to me to ask why my mother didn't come to visit. I just knew I was her "brave little man" by going.

When we got to the hospital, we were guided to the visitor's room. I noticed my father coming towards us. I wanted to go to him, but I held back. He looked strange. His hair was messed up, and he had small particles of food embedded in the corners of his mouth. His clothes hung on him, and he had a wild look in his eyes I had never seen before. We walked outside where it was more peaceful. But my father became more agitated.

"I don't get any rest here. This is a crazy house, and all I get are drugs and shots, and they're talking about shocking my brain. Get me the hell out of here. Jeezus, Harry, I just got a little depressed because I couldn't find work to support my wife and son. Is that a crime? Why the hell am I locked up here?"

Harry's voice was quiet. He got up, and he put his hand on my father's arm like he was gentling a frightened colt. "I'll talk to the doctors, I promise. Just calm down. I'm sure you'll get out soon."

I was confused and scared. Why was my father in this kind of place? What kind of place was this? Why did he call it a "crazy house?"

I visited my father for fifty-two excruciating Sundays with uncle Harry. I came to fear the tree tunnel as we approached Camarillo and I thought about the story of *Alice in Wonderland*.

"But I don't want to go among mad people," Alice remarked.

"Oh, you can't help that," said the Cat. "We're all mad here. I'm mad. You're mad."

"How do you know I'm mad?" said Alice.

"You must be," said the Cat, "or you wouldn't have come here."

My father's condition grew increasingly worse. On one of our visits, he seemed particularly agitated. He didn't seem to notice me standing beside my uncle. He finally looked at me with a blank stare. "Who's the kid with you, Harry?" I was devastated. My father didn't even know who I was.

I longed to have my father back, the one I had before he was put in the hospital, but he was gone, and I was alone. I grew up living with terrifying questions that I could never voice. What happened to my father? Would it happen to me? How could I become a man without the guidance of a dad?

1969: Are You Still Listening?

One day, during one of my uncle's visits, my father said he wanted to get some stamps at the post office. He walked across the street and disappeared. What happened to him is another story, one I write in my book, *My Distant Dad: Healing the Family Father Wound.*

In my mind, I can't separate my early experiences with my father in 1949 from my experiences becoming a father in 1969. So I'd like to return to my life in the second half of the 1960s.

When I began my graduate studies in 1965, I didn't know whether I was in favor of the war in Vietnam or opposed to it. So, I hired a graduate student who had studied the history of Vietnam and felt it was our duty to send troops there in support of freedom. I wanted him to educate me. But I also wanted to get another view, so I hired another graduate who seemed equally knowledgeable but felt we should not be fighting in Vietnam and we should stop sending troops and withdraw our support to a regime he felt was corrupt.

After hearing both sides, I joined the protests and marched for peace. I was beaten by Hells Angels when the Oakland police let them ride their motorcycles through the police lines to attack us. We were defenseless protesters who had sat in the street when the police prevented us from reaching the Oakland Army Terminal where young men were being sent to fight. After being tear-gassed by police, I became so outraged I wanted to kill the pigs. My rage frightened me. I knew I had to deal with my emotions if I was going to be an effective peace advocate.

When members of Synanon, a drug and alcohol treatment program for addicts, came to the Berkeley campus to offer "the game" (a form of intense confrontation and group therapy) to the students, I decided to join the "square game club," as it was called, and received a dual education. I learned from excellent teachers in the classroom and street-wise former addicts in Synanon. I learned to understand my anger better and to channel it into active advocacy rather than wanting to kill the cops.

[123]

My college sweetheart moved from U.C. Santa Barbara, where we had met, to U.C. Berkeley where I was in graduate school, and we got married in 1966. We didn't have time for a honeymoon until the following year when we went to Monterey. We didn't know that the Monterey Pop Festival was going on the same weekend, but jumped at the chance to hear some of the great musical acts of the day including The Jimi Hendrix Experience, The Who, Ravi Shankar, The Jefferson Airplane, The Mamas and the Papas, and Simon and Garfunkel singing "Homeward Bound" and their haunting anthem, "Sounds of Silence." But our absolute favorite was Janis Joplin, dazzling in white, opening her soul as she wailed about love and loss in "Ball and Chain."

We returned to school after the summer break, and I immersed myself in graduate school. One of my fellow students was Mel Newton, the brother of Huey P. Newton, who had co-founded the Black Panther Party with Bobby Seale. Although the Black Panthers started as peaceful advocates for human rights, police violence and attacks on the Panthers contributed to armed confrontations with the police. At a time when violent confrontations were the order of the day, Synanon was able to bring Panthers and Oakland Police together to leave their guns and engage each other in a non-violent confrontation in the Synanon game.

I still remember seeing Black Panthers, resplendent in their black leathers and Afros coming into the Synanon house in Oakland along with Oakland police with their bulging muscles and thick necks. It was a noble experiment that lasted for many months. It didn't bring peace, but it allowed conflicting groups to see each other as human beings and to express their anger, pain, and fear in an atmosphere of safety. It might have succeeded if the government had not decided that the Panthers were enemies of the State who needed to be eliminated.

In 1968, I graduated from U.C. Berkeley with a master's degree in Social Welfare and got my first job as a psychiatric social worker at Napa State Hospital. My hospital experiences brought back memories of my visits to see my father at Camarillo State Hospital so many years before. But things were changing in the field of mental health treatment. Therapeutic communities were beginning to emerge that were therapeutic and helpful and didn't rely on drugging the patients to treat them. By the beginning of 1969, I had started a therapeutic community for addicts based on what I had learned in Synanon.

During the summer of 1969, we had another musical experience that spoke deeply to our lives. In August, the American Conservatory Theater (ACT) put on the rock musical *Hair* at the Orpheum Theatre in San Francisco. The themes of war, the draft, protests, clean air, sex, friendship, betrayal, and love touched our souls. The songs— "Aquarius," "I Believe in Love," "I Got Life," "Easy to Be Hard," "Good Morning Sunshine"— opened our hearts. At the end of the performance, we joined the actors on stage where we held hands and sang to "let the sun shine" and bring on the Age of Aquarius.

Hair was a wonderful prelude to the event in November 1969 that forever changed my life. It began at another hospital, Kaiser Hospital in Vallejo. I'd been coaching my wife through the breathing exercises we learned in our Lamaze child-birthing classes. She'd been in labor more than 14 hours when the nurse announced, "It's time to move into the delivery room, Mrs. Diamond." My wife offered a wan smile and nodded her head.

The nurse then turned to me. "OK, Mr. Diamond, your job here is done. It's time for you to go to the waiting room." I was disappointed. I knew the rules of the hospital that didn't allow fathers into the delivery room, but I felt we had come this far together, and I wanted to go the whole way. However, I was a good Jewish boy who followed the rules, particularly those that affected my wife.

Even though I hadn't followed the rules in my political protests against the war in Vietnam, I kissed my wife on her cheek and squeezed her shoulder. "I'll see you and the baby soon," I assured her. As they wheeled her to the left towards the delivery room, I walked to the right towards the waiting room. But as I started to push through the doors, I couldn't go through them. Something stopped me. In my mind, I heard the voice of our unborn son calling to me. *I don't want a waiting room father. Your place is here with us.* I turned around and walked back the way I had come. The words kept reverberating in my mind. *I don't want a waiting room father.*

I walked through the delivery room door and took my place at the head of the table beside my wife. There was no question of leaving. Our son had called me, and I was there. Shortly after that, Jemal Eugene Diamond came into the world on November 21, 1969. He was handed to me amid tears of relief and joy. As I looked into his beautiful face, and our eyes met, I made a promise to him that I would be a different kind of father than my father was able to be for me. I would do everything I could to bring about a world where fathers were fully involved in the lives of their families from beginning to end.

In the years that followed, my wife and I fulfilled our dream that we had voiced while we were in college at U.C. Santa Barbara. "When we get married," we agreed in one of our serious discussions about our future, "let's have one child, then adopt a child." We both wanted children, but felt with so many people on the planet, the responsible thing to do would be to adopt a second child who needed a home.

In June 1972, we drove from our home in Stockton, California, to Los Angeles to meet the little girl, we eventually took home. She turned out to be a 2 ½-month-old, African-American baby. Her birth parents were just 15 years old, we were told. They loved their daughter but felt they couldn't give her the best home, so they agreed to make her available for adoption. I still remember the first time I held this little bundle of beauty. She looked into my eyes and smiled. I thought of my father and wondered if he'd ever meet his grandchildren. I remembered the promise I had made to be a different kind of father. We named our daughter Angela in honor of the place she was born and after the African-American political activist, Angela Davis, whom my wife and I had met in college and admired greatly.

Like her namesake, our Angela was a fighter. She was born with a cleft palate, and whenever she'd drink milk, it would go up into her nose, and she would choke—not a very comforting way to begin life. She had an operation to close the hole in her palate when she was a year old. The surgery was successful, but she was terrified to go to sleep, so afraid, I'm sure, that something bad would happen to her if she let her guard down. It took her years to sleep through the night and many more years of speech therapy to be able to develop her language skills. But she did grow up to become a woman I greatly admire.

The years rolled on. Our social activism continued, and the children marched with us, first in backpacks, then strollers, and finally they could walk beside us. My son, Jemal, still has a poster with "War is not healthy for children and other living things," in various languages. I finally found my lost father, and he did meet his grandchildren. My children grew up and had children of their own, and I continue to do my part to change the world. My father was a writer of poetry, plays, and prose. When he first met his grandchildren, he gave them a book of his poetry. The poems were full of love, pain, and promise. One that still runs through my mind when I think about my dad is called "Because of You."

Because of you

No longer stone,

I walk on puffs

Of clouds.

Because of you

Old madness

Has become

New meaning,

New purpose.

Because of you

My tongue

Is no longer

Lead

But song.

Because of you

Days are spangled

With stardust.

Nights are bright

With sun-glow.

Because of you

I want to live.

I miss you, Dad, and I miss the passion and promises of the 1960s. It's been said that "if you remember the '60s you weren't there." I disagree. I was there, and I'll never forget. I have a son who was born at the end of the '60s and a daughter who was born at the beginning of the '70s. I feel blessed to remember and doubly blessed to share the memories with you.

CHAPTER THIRTEEN

Flash of White

By Brent Green

A car hood appeared from nowhere at my waist level, as if it materialized out of nothingness. That's all I saw: a flash of white, a sense of being struck by something large and menacing, and then blank blackness.

After an unknown period of unconsciousness, two passersby helped me stand and escorted me toward a curb, my legs wobbly, my mind disoriented as to time and place. Rivulets of blood streamed down my face and covered my white T-shirt within seconds. Bystanders helped me sit while they summoned an ambulance. Other curious pedestrians gathered around me. I felt pressure on the top of my head as someone blotched my oozing blood with a towel. I looked up to see a confident young black woman who announced that she was a nurse. Dizzy and chastened by alarming awareness that I had been struck by a car, I could barely mutter, "Thank you."

I looked around to see a white VW Beetle and the driver's side exterior mirror laying on the pavement; that triggered a bottomless pain in my right rib cage. My gauzy vision also beheld a bearded man with shoulder-length hair and Benjamin Franklin glasses, dressed in a white suit. An angel? A saint?

No, my pragmatic mind decided, a human man like me. He held a blood-soaked towel to his head, his other arm around a tall, comely Scandinavian woman. They looked at me as they spoke with two bobbies.

As a curious tourist, I had learned that the "bobby" nickname for London police came from a derivation of Robert, inspired by the name of Sir Robert Peel (1778—1850), a politician who oversaw the creation of London's first organized police force. The man in the white suit commanded their attention, their expressions bright with approval. I couldn't identify him, but an eerie feeling that I knew him possessed me. Why is he so lovable? He had nailed me as I crossed a pedestrian crosswalk in the middle of a sunny day. That's not adorable.

London Ambulance Service arrived within minutes; a driver and paramedic appeared, quickly assessing my condition and helping me onto a stretcher. I looked again at the familiar figure of a man dressed in white, thinking of him as human but also perhaps a guardian angel. Could he have been a passenger in the VW that had almost flattened me in a zebra-stripe pedestrian crosswalk? I did not recall why I was there or how it could have happened that I had been hit by a car. The pain became unrelenting as the paramedic began connecting me with IVs.

"Going to be okay, mate," he reassured me in a thick Cockney accent. "I don't think you av broken bones." He introduced himself as Arthur and continued to assess my condition as the ambulance raced through traffic, siren screaming. Arthur spoke with me in reassuring tones while explaining everything he was doing to make me more comfortable with my escalating pain and sudden existential awareness, an unfathomable realization of being struck by a car. I had been looking left and right for cars since I could walk. I had walked tens of thousands of miles without even a close call. An accident couldn't have happened to me. Impossible.

1969: Are You Still Listening?

Pathetic?

Within minutes the ambulance pulled into an emergency room entrance. As Arthur and the ambulance driver wheeled me through a waiting area, I caught a glimpse of a sign hanging over the reception desk: The Hospital of Saint John and Saint Elizabeth. I had not heard of this hospital but realized it must be closest to the intersection where I had been hit. A bevy of medical personnel surrounded me as they pushed my stretcher into an examination room, tearing clothes off me and jabbering about their triage. They painfully transferred me from the ambulance stretcher to an examination table. My vision faded to grey and then featureless black. "He's drifting into unconsciousness—" I heard someone say.

LMW281F—

LMW281F—that was an alphanumeric swirling in my head when I came back to consciousness. I was lying prone in an emergency room on an examination table, surrounded by two nurses and a doctor. My vision was blurry, but I understood my circumstances. I looked up at a young nurse applying bandages to my head and spoke slowly: "L, M, W, 2, 8, 1, F..."

"What's he saying?" asked someone out of my field of vision.

"LMW281F," I said again. "Please help me remember." A male nurse approached me with a notepad and pen. "What was it again, sir?"

"L, M, W, 2, 8, 1, F," I answered in a tone of voice loud enough to be heard by anyone in the room.

"What does it mean?" asked the male nurse.

Wincing with pain in my lower ribcage and both knees, I said, "I don't remember, but it's important."

The next several days became a haze of medical tests, probing examinations by a horde of specialists, morphine for merciless pain, and drudgeries of hospital routine. Every hour on the hour, an intercom system announced a Catholic blessing, as if saints speaking. Not being Catholic but Protestant, I was initially offended by this not-so-subtle form of proselytizing, but, eventually, these announcements became comforting with predictability and then I listened to the heartening messages.

Late during the night of my third day in the hospital, I could not sleep, and I resisted shooting myself up with more morphine from a self-administering IV apparatus. All I needed to do was push a button to receive another dose of a warm and soothing liquid luring me into slumber, but I held back, trying to clear my thoughts. I still could not remember what happened exactly or identify occupants in the white VW—just images of a saintly man dressed in white, also bloodied by the car accident.

At 2:00 a.m., according to my watch on a nearby nightstand, the intercom system announced an hourly blessing:

Heavenly Father bless all those who are here for comfort and healing and fill them with new hope and strength. Relieve them of pain and sustain all the sick with your power. Lord, have mercy. We ask this through Christ our Lord. Amen.

My lips moved, silently forming "Amen." I needed hope and strength since I felt alone and isolated being far from family and friends in the States. I had no visitors other than hospital personnel. I had been told I would be released within a couple of days by my attending physician, Dr. Williams. But I needed first to gain strength and clear mental fogginess.

I could not sleep, and some higher moral calling inside me refused further anesthetic salvation through an opiate derivative. Instead, I tried to assemble in my mind what I remembered about the facts of my accident.

I recalled that I had taken the Underground from my hotel near Harrod's to St. John's Wood station. I had walked west on Grove End for approximately 500 meters and taken a right turn. Then I began to cross the street's zebra-stripe pedestrian walkway when a white VW struck me. I'm sure I looked both ways first, even with the protective reassurance of a pedestrian crosswalk giving me indisputable right-of-way. That's a pedestrian habit formed when I still barely knew how to walk, as a toddler.

I saw the vehicle but did not have time to react. Just the flash of a white hood then blackness and unconsciousness. No pain at first. My earliest memory is of sitting up in the middle of the crosswalk surrounded by strangers. My first conscious thought was disbelief that such a thing could have happened to me.

I watched instant-replay images of the minutes before and after the collision, sensing sad and complicated feelings about being a victim of such uncompromising blunt-force trauma. Then I saw my blood spilling onto my T-shirt and brief glimpses of bystanders, including the dude dressed in a white suit, also bloodied but in better shape than me.

What lessons could I learn from this? Never travel again? Always wear a dayglo jumpsuit? Not going to happen. Then I thought of a single word to sum up what I might take away from so much pain and interruption of the daily flow of my life as usual. *Vigilance*, a state of keeping a careful watch for possible dangers or difficulties, a traveling quality equally applicable to driving, cycling, or walking—here, there, and everywhere. Vigilance would become my mantra and rally cry going forward. I then submitted to agony clambering up a one-to-ten scale, edging closer to eight, and I activated the morphine injection machine to fall into a soft pillow of haze and forgetfulness—

Sunshine streamed into my room as I opened my eyes. Standing next to my bed was a man with Benjamin Franklin glasses and a long beard, wearing a faded denim shirt and dark blue jeans. I recognized him as the same character I had noticed five days earlier. Sitting in a chair near my bed was a Scandinavian woman who looked self-contained and complicated. She was beautiful with sunshine surrounding her platinum blond hair as if a halo.

The man said, "Ow's yur ed?"

I felt bandages encircling my head, rediscovering a wound and pain at the site of a large laceration near the center of my forehead. "Healing, I think." The man leaned closer as if to engage me in a private conversation. "There's no problem, only solutions. I'm ear ta elp."

A nurse's aide rushed into my room. "Do you want breakfast now?" she asked me.

"Maybe later. Coffee would be groovy."

The visitor standing next to my bed said, "Could you bring a spot uh tea?"

The aide reacted as if to say no, but then she realized something about the man, yet undefined to me. "Sure, of course." And to the Scandinavian woman, the nurse said, "And you also, mam? Tea?" The woman nodded "Yes, thank you. Herbal." The aide rushed out of the room, thrilled with a surprise encounter.

He reached for my hand and shook. "Winston O'Boogie—call me Winston," he said. "Call er Bridgette," he added, nodding at his partner.

I said, "You were involved in the accident, weren't you?"

He looked at his partner perhaps for some charitable understanding, took a deep breath, and answered, "I was driving the Beetle. It's not much of a car compared to me Austin Maxi, which was in the shop, and we needed some fast wheels to get to the studio. That Bug is a leftover treasure from me poverty days. I still love that car—"

"It was our first official recording day, and his mates were waiting," said the woman in her soft voice. "We were late for the session. Winston said he could drive, but I have always told him he's a lousy driver."

"She's right again," he said, "I am a wobbly driver." He paused, "Chauffeurs from now on. How are you feeling?"

I felt unrelenting pressure in my right rib cage where I had clipped off the VW's exterior mirror on the driver's side. My head pounded from a face-plant on the pavement. "Like shit. I can say for certain that my left calf muscle doesn't hurt."

"You're born in pain. Pain is what we are in most of the time, and I think that the bigger the pain, the more God you look for."

I glanced suspiciously at Bridgette who was nodding her head in agreement with Winston. "Are you saying that God is pain or pain is God?"

He sat on the edge of my bed next to my feet. "God is the concept by which we measure pain."

"My head is still pretty foggy, so I'm not tracking on everything right now. Help me out, Winston. Why are you here?"

His voice became lyrical as if singing a song. "I'm just sitting here watching the wheels go 'round. No longer riding on the merry-go-round. I just ad to let it go."

"You have an amazing voice! Bridgette mentioned a studio date. Are you a musician?"

He pulled assiduously on his long beard. "I'm interested in concepts an philosophies. I'm not interested in wallpaper, which most music is." He patted my left calf, the only part of my body not then throbbing.

"Have you had a close call with death, Winston?"

"I know what it's like to be dead, and I know what it is to be sad." He pulled back his long hair and pointed at a bandage covering his left ear. "Got that by hitting the window when I jerked the wheel and tried to dodge you."

I recalled then that he had also been injured in the accident. I tried to sit up, but he gently pushed my chest back to keep me lying down.

"Take it easy as it comes," Winston said. "I've been through it all, and nothing works better than to ave somebody you love old you."

A sudden weight of sadness fell over me, a realization again that I was both injured and alone, a *stranger in a strange land* as

Robert Heinlein wrote. Pushing those feelings into the background, I asked, "Will you return to the studio and record?"

Winston stared at Bridgette, his eyes full of love. "The dream is over. I'm talking about the generation thing. It's over, and we gotta get down to reality."

"Yes, I agree," I said, not quite sure what he meant. "Life is fragile and short. That much I have learned from all this."

"Fragile, short, and sometimes painful," added Bridgette, a luminous halo around her face, making her appear divine.

Winston backed away from my bed and nodded at Bridgette, signaling the time to leave. "This accident has lessons such as how to feel fear and pain. I can handle it better than I could before. I'm the same; only there's a channel. It doesn't just remain in me, and it goes round and out. I can move a little easier. I hope you can find this place also."

"As do I." After a thoughtful pause, I added, "I forgive you for hitting me. You are a man whose heart is filled with peace and love."

"That's all I'm saying nowadays: let's give peace a chance."

Winston and Bridgette moved nearer to the door. A sense of peacefulness washed over me, and I felt liberated from pain, anxiety, and uncertainty that arrived with my injuries.

Winston said, "When you get back, look us up. We're hanging at the studios for a few weeks to finish our business. Then we're off to Amsterdam."

"I'll leave your name with security," added Bridgette, handing me a business card with an address. "Don't be a loner. We're your friends now and let's get together when you can."

The celestial couple turned and seemed to float across my hospital room.

"I will," I answered. "Nothing's going to change my world if I don't." I thought for a second and then asked, "Winston, is your car license tag LMW281F?"

He turned to face me again and replied, "That is it, mate. How do you know this?"

"I don't know. I certainly don't have a photographic memory. It just came to me after I became conscious."

Winston looked at Bridgette and then at me. "I'll tell you what. Watch for our next album, and that number will be on the cover. It will become my private tribute to you. It's the least I can do—in addition to paying your medical bills and buying you some new cloves an stuff."

"What will be the title of the album?"

Winston glanced at Bridgette for a thoughtful pause. "There won't be a title. The only type on the cover will be on a license tag attached to my Beetle. We'll get her fixed up just for the photo shoot."

"What will people call the album without a title?"

Winston snickered as if he had just invented a devious prank. "It will be known by where we created and recorded it, nothing more."

"And that is?"

"The pedestrian crossing where I hit you. Abbey Road."

Tailpiece

This chapter is an interesting blend of creative imagination and nonfiction. The story evolved from Brent's real-life experience of being hit by a car near his home in Denver, Colorado, when he was crossing a pedestrian crosswalk. The car accident imagery described in this story is consistent with his experiences, including a trip by ambulance to a hospital emergency room, although without a hospital stay.

Dr. Winston O'Boogie was John Lennon's favorite nickname. It is also true that Lennon was a lousy driver, and on July 1, 1969, he steered his white British Leyland Austin Maxi into a ditch near Durness, Scotland, in the Highlands. Lennon, his son Julian (with first wife Cynthia Lennon), Yoko Ono and Ono's daughter, Kyoko, sustained minor injuries. They were taken to

Lawson Memorial Hospital in Golspie. Julian was treated for shock. Lennon, Ono, and Kyoko received stitches to repair facial lacerations. Pregnant at the time, Ono also sustained minor back injuries.

Abbey Road was the eleventh studio album created by the English rock band and penultimate album ever written and recorded by The Beatles. Apple Records released the LP in September 1969. These studio sessions were also the final times all four Beatles worked together simultaneously in their beloved Abbey Road Studios, located at 3 Abbey Road, London. The album was hailed by TIME magazine as "one of the most acclaimed rock albums in history."

On an album cover without a traditional title, the four Beatles cross an intersection in single file in a now-famous pedestrian crosswalk. Lennon is wearing a white suit. The only typography to be seen on the cover is a license plate attached to an iconic Volkswagen Beetle, owned by one of the neighborhood residents. That license plate number, LMW281F, has also taken on mythological proportions. Bridgette, the Scandinavian woman posing as Winston's partner in the story, is fictitious, conceived by the author so as not to tip off readers too early in the story by describing and even naming Ono.

CHAPTER FOURTEEN

Guns, Wings, & Rites of Passage

By Robert William Case

Be it remembered that liberty must against all hazards be supported. We have the right to it derived from our Maker...Let us dare to read, think, speak, and write.

— John Adams,
2nd U.S. President 1797-1801

What is your coming of age story?

In 1969, my family lived in the city of Akron, Ohio, a few miles away from the small farming community of Kent. Route 59 wound through verdant countryside, joining this village of 30,000, not counting the university students, with the industrial city where I grew up and went to public school.

The two-lane black-top road led past barns and farmhouses, pastures and hayfields. In Springtime white blossomed dogwood trees accented the yards and hillsides. This was my hometown, that place for beginnings, for learning from family and community the lessons of who "I am."

In 1969, I was seventeen, a young Icarus much like the one in Greek mythology. I was eager to test my wings. One more year to go before emancipation, or at least high school graduation and college. One year to go before registering for the draft. That summer, while I washed dishes and bused tables at a local restaurant, Woodstock happened. It promised to be a thrilling senior year. My older brother was finally leaving for college. I would finally have my own bedroom.

Our northeast Ohio home was both crucible and nest. The war in Vietnam was churning through lives and bodies on both sides at a rapid clip. Even without twenty-four-hour news, the outside world was in a constant state of unrest. With each year of my growing awareness, U.S. involvement in that faraway place ratcheted up another notch. In the innocence of my inner world, I was having flight dreams. My favorite was the one that began in the middle of a peaceful meadow on top of a grassy hill, the sun, directly overhead. I raised my arms like a great winged bird, lifted one leg, went into a spin, and then, gravity released me. I rose above the fields to soar on the winds wherever they would take me. I wanted to be more than just another kid from Akron bent on leaving the troubled economy of the Rust Belt behind.

In 1969, my grandfather was in failing health, but still carrying on the family farm with a few tired dairy cows. I can remember damming up a small stream deep in the woods and then breaching it to unleash a mighty torrent, all the way to the Little Mahoning Creek. I remember the damp, musky smell of the woods in Autumn, the sound of leaves underfoot. Sometimes it felt like I had one foot in the city and the other on the farm. Grandpa taught me what it meant to be a good hunter, to only need one shot. Besides, ammunition for his bolt action, .22-calibre varmint rifle cost money. He didn't have that much. At fifteen, I had the arms and shoulders of a young man who knew the finer points of baling hay. Grandpa drove the tractor. Jim from a nearby farm showed me how to stack a hay wagon high and tight. We were in the same grade at different schools. We had everything in common, except for his height and the size of his tanned forearms.

There is a soul-satisfying enrichment from being rooted in the land. My siblings and I still own the farm. It's been in our family for five generations. One of our grandfathers bought the original one hundred acres after his discharge from the Union Army at the end of the Civil War. He was a corporal in the 206th Regiment of Pennsylvania Volunteers, discharged in Richmond, Virginia on June 26, 1865, and with no place to go except home. I know these details because his discharge papers are framed and mounted on the wall of my home office. My sister Pat has an old black and white photograph of him and his wife with their youngest son. Someone in my family has farmed that land ever since, including me.

In 1969, we lived in a time and place where law and culture coalesced to pressure healthy young men like Jim and me into college or the military or to jail. The only other path was exile to Canada. Jim didn't want to go to college. He didn't want to go to war half-way across the globe either. He wanted very much to stay right there and farm and get serious with his high school sweetheart. But he felt real pressure to enlist, the potential for real shame if he didn't. His dad and the other fathers around Smicksburg had their own war to talk about. Even if they didn't like talking about it all that much.

1969 was the second year of a five-year prison sentence imposed on a well-known Olympian from Louisville, Kentucky. Evading the draft was a federal crime. Cassius Clay was the subject of praise and approval around our midwestern dinner table after winning Olympic gold in 1960 for boxing. No one noticed in 1964 when he failed to qualify for military service because of insufficient reading and writing skills. But as the war escalated the Selective Service lowered its eligibility standards to meet rising demand. Reclassified 1-A, he applied for conscientious objector status as a member of the Black Muslim faith. The draft board denied his request. In 1967, he received his notice to appear for induction. He fully complied with a required appearance but refused to step forward after his name was called. Immediately, he was charged with draft evasion.

The sound of a man falling from the pedestal of Olympic glory swept across the Midwest. "How can a professional fighter claim to be a conscientious objector?" The logic went around in circles at our family dinner hour.

Muhammad Ali responded with his trademark verbal acuity, exposing the fault lines in our Midwestern values. He demanded a jury trial. Ultimately, he was found guilty, sentenced to five years in jail, fined $10,000, and stripped of his heavyweight title. But the jail-time was suspended, pending an appeal to the next higher court.

Speaking of pressure, I was a geeky, nearsighted high school kid in the city. Far too shy for talking with girls, I read a lot of books. My teachers expected me to go to college. So did my parents. "Are you getting those college applications in?" my father regularly inquired. College, with its student deferment, was for him the only sensible course. To me, it was the path of least resistance, the acceptable way to avoid going to Vietnam. What could be safer than going to college in the Midwest?

As a seventeen-year-old high school senior, the capricious ways of the draft were a constant source of interest. The Selective Service operated under the sole discretion of the executive branch. In the face of declining popularity, Nixon gave it a facelift in 1969 by changing the draft into a lottery system. The first drawing was held on December 1st. Within its eligibility pool were budding young notables like Bruce Springsteen, Bill Murray, and Brent Green, and future presidents Bill Clinton, George W Bush, and Donald Trump.

The drawing was televised to a national audience during primetime. I don't remember watching. Seventeen and politically naïve, I was still increasingly dissatisfied with the way the war was going. This was not a position my parents cared to hear. Growing up in our Midwestern home, I never heard either one of them find fault with the war or the increasing costs in money and lives. They wanted it to end, but with honor. That was the promise the president had made to garner their votes the year before. They would approve of whatever he proposed to carry out this nebulous plan. If they had any doubts, they were never expressed within hearing range of my ears. What they did express quite openly was their disdain for anyone protesting it.

Graduating from high school during a time of war was something Dad and I shared in common. On the day Pearl Harbor was attacked, he was a freshman at Ohio University, studying to become a dentist. Dad was drafted right away. The Army put him in an ROTC uniform and left him in school. That was 1941. But after battles like Guadalcanal were fought and won, wounded soldiers and sailors from the Pacific began overflowing into stateside hospitals for long-term care and treatment. To meet the demand, Dad was converted into an Army medic to work as an orderly at the military hospital in Dayton, Ohio. He cared for its gravely wounded survivors for the rest of the war. In 1945, he was discharged a First Lieutenant.

Although Dad never served in a combat zone, he had no illusions about the damage inflicted during combat upon the human body and spirit. With all that in his resume, the closest he could come to being critical of the war in Vietnam was to say to my older brother as he went away to college in 1969, "I spent enough time in uniform for all of us. You shouldn't have to go." I did not doubt that Dad included me in that statement. There was no other way to make sense of a world that wouldn't let me choose my own way.

Many others were finding reasons to oppose the war. The issue came into sharp focus on April 30th, 1970, in an evening television address. Nixon announced the invasion of Cambodia by 20,000 American and South Vietnamese troops. I would graduate in one month. He called it an "incursion." The *New York Times* called it a "virtual renunciation" of his promise to end the war. Even the conservative *Wall Street Journal* took a stand, warning against deeper entrapment in Southeast Asia.

The next day protests erupted on university and college campuses across the nation. One of them was Kent State University (KSU), so close to my backyard.

Kent was an old mill town in the middle of farm country, with the usual assortment of banks and businesses, straddling the Cuyahoga River. In my seventeen-year-old view of the world, it was like a magnet, the only place to go for 3.2 beer on my upcoming eighteenth birthday. It was well known that the best bars were all on Water Street. My view of Kent was soon to change.

About 11:00 p.m. that day, warm Spring temperatures combined with alcohol and antiwar sentiments to inspire a crowd of young people to swarm onto Water Street. They closed it down with their numbers, blocking a meaningful police response. The crowd set bonfires, defaced storefronts, and broke windows. As the night wore on, city police broke up and dispersed the crowd. After reviewing the scene and listening to rumors of radical plots, the mayor and police chief declared a state of emergency.

On Saturday, the mayor telephoned the governor for assistance. It was a quiet day full of rumors and speculation, but once darkness fell about six-hundred people gathered on the Commons, the traditional place for pep rallies, frisbees, and peaceful public assemblies. A rickety old Army ROTC building stood close by. Novelist James Michener, in his nonfiction work published in 1971, *Kent State: What Happened and Why*, wrote that, regrettably, the KSU police did nothing to disperse the crowd gathered on the Commons, even as burning matches were tossed onto the wooden structure for almost an hour before it finally started to smolder and burn.

Once it was going, the fire department sirens brought out additional spectators, but still no response by university police. Fire crews arrived and were pelted with rocks. Their hoses were slashed—but still no response by KSU police. Without a police response, there was nothing for the battered crew to do but pack up their truck and go home, leaving the Commons to the mob. They were still there around midnight when the guard arrived and began clearing the campus with tear gas and armed patrols.

By midmorning on Sunday, one thousand national guard troops were on hand to greet James Rhodes, Governor of Ohio. He held a morning press conference with city officials. Intending to motivate both troops and voters, he declared a state of emergency. He went on to describe protesters as "the worst sort of people we harbor in America," directing the Guardsmen to "use every weapon possible to eradicate the problem."

Rhodes was not alone in his combative approach. He was following the lead of Ronald Reagan, then governor of California, who in an April 7th speech to constituents concerning student unrest had declared, "If it takes a bloodbath, let's get it over with. No more appeasement."

Sunday was warm and pleasant on the KSU campus. Michener described it as a carnival atmosphere. Sightseers from as far away as Cleveland and Akron made the trip to Portage County to visit the ruins of the ROTC building. Traffic into Kent was backed up for miles. Young people were out in spring attire, some of the women flirting with the soldiers. One of them was Allison Krause, who achieved fame and portent that afternoon by placing a delicate yellow flower into the muzzle of a guardsman's rifle.

The carnival atmosphere came to an end in the twilight of the 8:00 p.m. curfew. As patrons and sightseers headed for home, Sunday night collapsed into another show of force and defiance between Guardsmen and the students. In his 2016 book, *67 Shots: Kent State and the End of American Innocence*, Howard Means writes that although individual soldiers carried vintage 30-caliber semi-automatic M-1 rifles, their supporting hardware was state of the art. This included helicopters and seven APC M113's, the fully tracked armored personnel carriers used in Vietnam for busting through the heavy jungle overgrowth.

Late morning on Monday was warm and clear. I was daydreaming my way through class, a senior with only a few more weeks to go before graduation. Six hundred guardsmen patrolled the campus, and regular classes were underway at KSU. Four hundred more were deployed in the city. Across the world, U.S. troops were fighting in Cambodia in an undeclared war. Normal scheduling meant that classes ended at 11:45 a.m. Then, the Commons would fill with several thousand students and staff, most of them heading to the union for lunch, back to their dorms, or even to another class.

About two hundred students gathered on the Commons near the victory bell in anticipation of a noon protest. It was time for Brigadier General Robert Canterbury, field commander of the Ohio National Guard, to add his name to the historical record by declaring to reporters, "These students are going to have to find out what law and order are all about."

Just before noon, the Commons began filling with students and passersby. A KSU police officer climbed into a jeep with two soldiers. They drove back and forth across the Commons, calling through a bullhorn, "This assembly is unlawful! The crowd must disperse! This is an order!"

Demonstrators by the victory bell responded with: "Power to the people! Pigs off campus!" and "One, two, three, four, we don't want your fucking war!"

"For your safety, all bystanders and innocent people, leave!" pleaded the police officer from the jeep.

Some started to disperse. Most did not. Canterbury determined that it was riot enough. He ordered his troops to lock and load their weapons, and to clear the Commons. Armed with live ammunition, the first wave of guardsmen advanced across the green field into a confused and incredulous crowd. Frightened students responded with shouts of fear or rage. Soldiers fired tear gas into the warm Ohio sunshine. More guardsmen advanced into the chaos. Students turned and fled, some even stopped to pick up a rock or even a pebble to throw at the advancing riflemen.

Students fled in the direction of Blanket Hill, a broad grassy knoll next to Taylor Hall where couples traditionally spread blankets and watch stars on warm spring nights. Canterbury ordered the seventy members of G troop to follow them. Their line of march took them past beyond the small hill and to the edge of a practice football field. There, a chain link fence blocked any further advance. The soldiers began regrouping. To their left, in front of Taylor Hall, a large crowd of students gathered, fascinated by the unfolding drama. To the right, a smaller band filled the Prentice Hall parking lot. Students and soldiers were close enough to feel the fear, see the anger: two disparate masses of young people, many sharing the same goal of avoiding service in Vietnam, and yet repelling each other like magnets of the same polarity.

The main body of guardsmen began retracing their steps toward Blanket Hill. Sensing a retreat, students on the Prentice Hall parking lot began to jeer. Several soldiers knelt and raised their rifles but did not fire. Frightened students gave way, making a path for the heavily armed men.

As the Guardsmen moved back toward the Commons, an unarmed eighteen-year-old student named Joseph Lewis approached them, overflowing with youthful fire and calling out his rage. It was such a spectacle—so derivative of the spirited defiance shown by an unarmed patriot at the Boston Commons exactly two hundred years before—that it caught the eye of news photographer John Darnell. From his perch on Blanket Hill, he captured a series of black and white photos that would soon stun a world audience, including that moment when a full platoon of twenty-eight soldiers turned in unison to form a skirmish line and face off with the jeering students. They raised their weapons as one and fired as a synchronized unit, sixty-seven bullets in thirteen seconds, all responding to the same silent directive. Some fired into the air; others fired into the ground. But, eight guardsmen fired directly into the crowd; all except for Sgt. Larry Schaefer. He aimed at the advancing figure of Joseph Lewis, middle finger raised in angry defiance and shot him in the stomach from sixty feet away.

The first fatality that day was Allison Krause, the young woman with the flower, killed by a bullet entering her left side from 330 feet away. Sandy Scheuer was next, walking with a friend and away from the conflict on her way to an afternoon class. She was killed by a bullet that struck her in the neck from 390 feet away. Third was William Schroeder, an honor student in geology and an Army ROTC cadet. The bullet that killed him entered the left side of his back, also from 390 feet away. The fourth fatality was Jeffrey Miller, shot in the face from just 270 feet away.

Student photographer John Filo was on that same parking lot. He stopped to take a picture of Jeffrey Miller and the huge volume of blood flowing from his gaping head wound. As he focused his camera, a young teenage runaway ran into the frame and dropped to one knee over the dead student. Filo captured the Pulitzer Prize-winning moment.

1969: Are You Still Listening?

From my lessons in Akron's public schools, I was well-versed in the historic event of March 5, 1770, in which an innocent gathering of unarmed colonials paid a heavy price for pelting a squad of British soldiers on the Boston Commons with snowballs. The bloody British opened fire with single-shot muzzleloaders, killing five and injuring six more. John Adams, then a young Boston attorney, declared it a massacre. Then he used it, fueled with his own strong beliefs in liberty, to promote rebellion from England and the noble cause of American independence.

So, I was not surprised the next day at school to see fellow students wearing black armbands in sympathy with the students at KSU. I carpooled that morning with friends from the neighborhood. We arrived early. Inside the front door was a larger than life bronze bust of Harvey Firestone. Behind him, a large high-ceilinged room also called the Commons, a place where we gathered before the opening bell. The room was electric with the roar of student voices, pulsing with energy, everyone focused on the same question, 'Was the shooting justified?' Occasional shoving matches rippled through the crowded space but no one intervened. How could anyone not have an opinion?

As graduation approached, I found myself sympathizing more and more with the KSU students. Every day the media rehashed the events with the latest developments. What most troubled my adolescent brain was the absence of pictures of injuries among the soldiers. If protesters had struggled with guardsmen to wrestle their weapons from them—if Guardsmen were in fear for their lives or bodily harm—then where were their torn uniforms, the bruises, or the bloody noses? All that I saw were pictures of injured students and interviews with traumatized parents.

Seventeen and politically naïve, I did know the difference between right and wrong. The distinction was drilled into me throughout childhood. As a preschooler on a shopping trip with my mother, I once stole a shiny pen and pencil set from a gift store. When she discovered the theft a few days later, I was immediately dragged back to the store sobbing and weeping, required to return the stolen item and apologize to the owner.

She believed just as strongly that the National Guard had the high moral ground. Even though I outweighed her by at least fifty pounds, I still remember the day she took me to task for comparing the shootings at KSU to the Boston massacre.

"Wham!" Came the sound of her open hand slamming against the kitchen counter, cutting me off in midsentence. "They were throwing bags of shit at those guardsmen!" she declared, articulating words with righteous fire.

"Who?" I asked, standing up to her five foot nothing in height.

"The ones who got shot!"

"How do you know that, Mom?" I asked, pressing the point. "Why aren't there any pictures of shit-covered guardsmen?"

"I heard it on the radio!" She fumed, jamming her finger into my chest. "It's in the papers. The governor said so."

"The one that's under investigation for tax evasion?"

"The Governor of Ohio!" she screamed again, the finger still pushing.

Dad was of a similar mind, without the emotion. "Maybe there should be an investigation," he opined. "But, if J Edgar Hoover doesn't have a problem with it, neither do I."

Seventeen was an appropriate age for arguing with my parents and questioning their authority. But I had more going on than just hormones. What had begun as a slight fever and ache in my back, was becoming a promising itch passing up and down my spine, and back and forth between my shoulder blades. I wanted badly to fly away from the safety and predictability of my childhood home. My wings were starting to develop.

My parents were both educated people, the first from their families to go to college. For them, supporting the troops was a sacred duty burned deep into their bones by the challenges and sacrifices of their war. Even with two teenage sons approaching draft age, with National Guard troops shooting down university students a few miles away, neither of my middle-aged parents could in good conscience deviate from those beliefs, so long defended. And, they were not alone. In one nationwide poll conducted after the KSU shooting, 58 percent of Americans believed that the Guard had done the right thing. Only 12 percent opined that the shootings were unjustified.

Sadly, in 1969, the voting age was still twenty-one.

On May 4th, University President Robert White closed KSU down. He sent the students home, told employees to stay home until further notice, and called for a full investigation. On Friday the last of the guardsmen left campus. So, if the National Guard was deployed to keep the university open, then clearly the mission failed. As they moved out, hundreds of FBI agents moved in. They set up temporary offices in one of the gymnasiums to gather and sift through evidence. The results would be compiled into a single report covering 7,500 typewritten pages, kept under lock and key in Washington and available to no one, except for multiple official commissions with authority to subpoena them. There were hundreds of adroit reporters trying to penetrate the wall of secrecy. It wouldn't take long before something was leaked.

Across the nation, impatient youth were not waiting for official commissions or their findings. On May 5th, student strikes erupted in bigger, more important cities with more significant universities than our rustic KSU, and with more influential alumni. So, if Canterbury's personal goal was to teach students a lesson about law and order, then clearly, he failed too. After the KSU shootings, National Guard units were mobilized on twenty-one campuses in sixteen states. Some were peaceful protests. Others were not. H. R. Haldeman, in his 1978 memoir about his years in the Nixon White House, *The Ends of Power*, identifies Kent State as the turning point in the presidency of

Richard Nixon, the "beginning of his downfall slide into Watergate."

I graduated from high school into a summer of unrest. I tried marijuana for the first time. It was a season to hibernate and take comfort in friends and food. My country friend Jim still hung around the farm. But he wouldn't consider letting the lottery decide his fate for him. "There's no pride in it," he would explain. Jim would rather enlist and give a gift of talking points to his family and community. The waiting list to join the Navy was long, the enlistment four years. For the National Guard, even longer.

On July 23, 1970, our local newspaper, the *Akron Beacon Journal*, broke the story on the results of the massive FBI investigation. It was a summary, a fourteen-page analysis prepared by a Director in the Justice Department. I still remember two of its significant points: The shootings were not necessary, and, flying rocks or projectiles hurt no guardsmen on May 4th.

I was sure that the results were sensational. Instead, the impact was like a fart in the wind. No one seemed to notice, except J. Edgar Hoover, then director of the FBI. He wrote a scathing letter to the editor, charging the paper with distorting the facts, and tersely stating that the results of his investigation were turned over to the Justice Department "without recommendation or conclusion."

Summer came to an end, and I left for college. Jim left on a bus for Alameda, California, and sea duty on the USS Ranger. People said that it was a new class of aircraft carrier, the kind with a split deck. Grandpa died that Winter near the land he loved.

Those first years at Allegheny College were my chrysalis years. I took classes without much ambition or direction. In the safety of my cocoon, the wings were growing. I read a lot, hung out at the student union, and listened to music. I also found a mentor in an unexpected place, a young professor in the German language department named Jurgen Richter. His stories about growing up in postwar Europe kindled a fire in me to go and experience travel for myself.

1971 was an auspicious year. On March 10th, the USS Ranger set a fleet record for launching flight sorties against bombing targets in North Vietnam, and, on June 7th returned to California for an overhaul. On July 28th, the U.S. Supreme Court unanimously overturned Muhammad Ali's conviction for draft evasion. (See *Clay v. the United States*, 403 U.S. 698 (1971)). His boxing license had been reinstated the year before. And on August 5th, the draft lottery for American men born in 1952 was finally held.

Jim was number 114, a grey zone regarding the likelihood of being called up. For him, it was a moot point. For me, I was effectively out of the draft, number 300! Like Donald Trump and Bill Clinton before me, numbers 356 and 311 respectively, I won a jackpot. At college, I was drifting in a slow current, letting others write the story of my life. This lottery result felt like a large fracture appearing on the inside wall of my cocoon. My wings were beginning to burst through. By spring and the end of the school year, they would be ready for testing. I had to start planning for the launch.

With the assistance of Professor Richter and others in the department, I applied for summer jobs and a visa to Germany. Open-ended, roundtrip tickets from New York to Luxembourg were for sale on Icelandic Airlines, good for up to one year. There were several thousand dollars in my bank account—from working part-time jobs since I was old enough to sling newspapers—waiting to be put to good use.

When classes ended that Spring, I was ready to launch, I dropped out of college and flew east, into the light and warmth of the sun. There was a job waiting for me with a construction company in Hamburg, Germany. It would be a total emersion. Out of the blue, Jim came to Cleveland Hopkins Airport to see me off. His Pittsburg Pirates baseball cap was gone, traded in for the Giants. He was on extended leave. Ranger was still in dry dock. Acts of sabotage by crewmembers were extending her stay. The latest, an industrial paint scrapper dropped into the main reduction gear (people say, that's something like the transmission on a car). Jim did not want to go back for the next cruise. He was thinking about leaving for Canada or even coming with me to Europe. His family was pressuring him not to quit. We had to say goodbye at the airport.

I spent a rewarding summer immersed in the language, commerce, and culture of Germany. Then, I traveled; throughout Europe and the Mediterranean, by thumb and backpack, working, falling in love, and beginning a study of philosophy and myth that continues to inform my writing and inspire my life. The year abroad was a self-administered rite of passage, a process that transformed me from dependent youth into a free-thinking man—and the prodigal son. Travel opened my eyes and reopened my heart after the bloodshed at KSU.

According to Mark Twain: "Travel is fatal to prejudice, bigotry, and narrow-mindedness, and many people need it sorely on these accounts. Broad wholesome, charitable views—cannot be acquired by vegetating in one little corner of the earth all one's lifetime." After a year of it, I was ready to reconnect with family and come home.

I believe that the ancient Greeks had it right all along; wings are the preferred tool for emancipating youth. In their mythology, Icarus had the good fortune of custom-made wings, built by a caring father, an inventor named Daedalus. Even if the father's warning was ineffective—the one about not flying too high—Icarus had his father's blessing. Daedalus did his best to emancipate his son well.

Thirty years later, I would be the one with teenage children. From our home in the western mountains, we traveled back to

Akron on vacation and went hiking together on a trail through one of the many metropolitan parks. The trail led through tall trees past an old limestone quarry, one whose stones helped build the Ohio Canal. The vertical face of the quarry wall was cut into a series of eight-foot ledges. Grandpa and I watched while the children climbed all over it. Try as he might, the younger sibling wasn't tall enough, to jump high enough to get his hand over the ledge with enough purchase to pull himself up to the next level.

Disappointed and frustrated, he took a break and came towards us. It was a multi-generational moment. "You've got such strong arms and legs," my dad observed, putting an arm around his shoulder. "That wall seems impossible, doesn't it?"

Ben nodded.

"Have your dad bring you back next year," he said, winking in my direction. "We'll take on these quarry walls again. I guarantee that you will like the results. You might even be impressed with how easily change can happen if you give it time."

To those places and themes, we did return the very next year. Ben has never forgotten those times with his Grandpa. And, when I needed a good story to include in my Dad's eulogy, that's the one I told. There wasn't a dry eye in the place.

CHAPTER FIFTEEN

Postscript: Reflections on Kent State

By Brent Green and Bob Moses

For decades, critics have discredited the Vietnam antiwar movement and its associated social uprisings. There were no antiwar movement heroes. It was a destructive rebellion, a rip in the fabric of democratic idealism, an unfortunate collision of youth, a generation out of control without traditional moral bearings. It was a time of adolescent upheaval, situational morality, and excesses of a free society. The predominant media narrative remembers drug experimentation, sexual promiscuity, mean-spirited disobedience—a volatile generation gap and a deviation from *the good social order* typically associated with the 1950s.

Baby Boomers and activist members of the Silent Generation, these critics remind us, abandoned the mainstream moral consensus. Instead, they chose self-gratification, marijuana, Woodstock, draft card burn-ins, and reckless and feckless protest marches. They turned America upon itself. The only accurate moral reflection upon the late sixties and early seventies was as a period of national disgrace.

The war may have been illegal (being undeclared by Congress), but not necessarily immoral. American soldiers bravely sacrificed to stop the spread of communism and save the indigenous Vietnamese from China's agenda of East Asian domination. Belligerent domestic disunity served no greater purpose than to encourage a tyrannical enemy, buttress Hanoi's resolve to fight harder, and beget dishonorable defeat. The most significant costs were borne by American soldiers: a tragic body count and enduring emotional trauma (e.g., PTSD) and physical injuries among thousands of surviving veterans. The best American citizens might hope for fifty years hence is to put the nightmarish mistakes of Vietnam behind us. Bury the memories.

Regrettably, this view marginalizes millions of Americans who stood firm against an undeclared war and an "enemy" that posed no direct threat to the U.S. It fails to recognize the power of democratic mobilization to alter the destiny of a nation and to protect the rights of citizens. It may even justify oppression or violence today against those who dare to challenge authority or popular opinion, their Constitutional right of free speech and human liberties notwithstanding.

President Richard Nixon called young protesters bums. Vice President Spiro Agnew labeled them "an effete corps of impudent snobs who characterize themselves as intellectuals." Social psychologist Bruno Bettelheim castigated youthful protests as lacking any serious political content. Concisely framing this perspective on the sixties, *Washington Post* conservative columnist Jonathan Yardley wrote this searing denunciation in a 1987 op-ed column: "The sixties had almost nothing to do with genuine ideological commitment or sense of purpose." Instead, he wrote, the sixties were "adolescent rebellion masquerading as a political movement."

1969: Are You Still Listening?

Those with vivid memories of the Kent State shootings must reel at the diminution of the sixties' antiwar protesters as destructive and devoid of higher purpose. The great majority of protesters embraced nonviolent protest while opposing racism, poverty, and the mutilating and untethered American bombardment of Vietnam. The universal obligation felt by antiwar protesters was to stop a heinous and undeclared war.

Half-a-century later, many living Americans do not recall this war's devastating impact. Vietnam incurred the death of more than 58,000 American men and women with over 300,000 wounded. The body count and suffering did not end with U.S. military casualties. During the war, the U.S. dropped 6.7 million tons of bombs on Indochina—including Vietnam, Laos, and Cambodia. The Vietnamese countryside, home to an ancient way of life, became the earth's most heavily bombed landscape, having more high explosives released upon it than on all the countries involved in World War II. American actions (based on the 1995 official Vietnam estimate of war dead) killed as many as 2 million Vietnamese civilians and some 1.1 million North Vietnamese and Vietcong fighters between 1965 and 1974. The 1972 Christmas bombing campaign ordered by President Richard Nixon made Hanoi the most heavily bombed city in the history of warfare up to that point. This was nearly two years *after* the bellwether incident when public opinion began its decisive turn against the war effort.

Yes, Kent State. On Monday, May 4, 1970, at 12:25 p.m., 28 National Guardsmen equipped with loaded M-1 rifles fired from the crest of Blanket Hill near Taylor Hall on the campus of Kent State University. They shot into a crowd of students gathered in the Prentice Hall parking lot. Many students were passing between classes during lunch hour. Guardsmen fired 67 shots in 13 seconds. They killed four students and injured nine others.

This unprecedented violence by the National Guard against unarmed college students became an epochal milestone in the history of the Vietnam War—just as the bombing of Pearl Harbor was to the WWII generation. Sixties' detractors should not ignore that social and political changes birthed in the sixties were advanced in significant measure by the Kent State shootings—a wake-up call for the nation that also harbingered a turning point in the war.

In 1971, following a nationwide strike by more than a half million high school, college and university students and faculty, Congress (with a 94-0 vote in the U.S. Senate) lowered the voting age from 21 to 18, giving young people a chance to vote for or against the politicians and policies impacting their lives. In 1973, Congress enacted the War Powers Act, limiting the authority of a U.S. president to usher America into an undeclared war. Behind a cloak of government secrecy and cover-up, covert invasions of Cambodia ended in August of the same year, seven months following the signing of the Paris Peace Accords on January 27. According to President Nixon's aide, H. R. Haldeman, Kent State was the beginning of Nixon's downhill slide to a disgraced resignation.

Boomers and others who stood firm against a tidal wave of popular pro-war public opinion influenced major social and political changes that endure now. Sadly, despite the War Powers Act, the impulse to participate in lengthy military actions without Congressional approval remains largely unrestrained, ignored by both Congress and the executive branch. On another side of the ledger, today we live in a society whose governmental institutions and private employers are less likely to treat women as second-class citizens. Racial minorities are less likely to suffer government-sanctioned policies of segregation and discrimination. Companies that dump contaminants and poisons into the environment do so at their peril.

Over time, the rebellious boys and girls of the sixties have been instrumental in making *all of this* happen. In the longer view of history, the shift of consciousness that emanated from the sixties has had, and will continue to have, far more impact on the U.S. future and the preservation and advancement of individual freedoms worldwide than our regrettable and tragic misadventure in Vietnam.

"The struggle of man against power is the struggle of memory against forgetting," philosopher Milan Kundera once observed. Love or hate the sixties' activists, we can still observe how a vocal and idealistic generation moved the Vietnam War toward conclusion, U.S. social and economic policies toward inclusion, and freedom of expression to new and uproarious heights.

CHAPTER SIXTEEN

A Sizzling Dream of Imagination

By Brent Green

I awake in a dream. It is 1969. I see a tapestry of images woven with careless haircuts, stringy recording tape, practical German cars, streets packed with singing protesters, and tattered denim jeans. I gobble sloppy cheeseburgers, sip thick black coffee, smoke random cigarettes, and sometimes slam down shots of Madeira wine. Burned car oil, sandalwood incense, cherry vodka, and chunky peanut butter with strawberry jam—these emblematic fragrances waft through my nostrils, burrowing into deep memory.

I think about differences and similarities but mostly differences, grasping for understanding of those who live momentous lives in daily desperation—history's awesome change agents willing to stand up and be counted.

My eyes squint, watering with unrest, darting with distrust, full of fuzzy fantasies about *a more perfect union* we have been promised. Instead, I become aware of dark shades of doubt rippling through society. I mentally challenge anyone who doesn't understand my misgivings about sit-com perfection, a televised world of white-folk tidiness and happier days ahead.

Demands placed upon me to make momentous career decisions are exasperating, especially in chaotic times. I want to fit neatly, to become a fundamental cog in the great machine of society, to enlist in the American Gleam Team. Nevertheless, I distrust conformity and bromides. I cannot be moored to safe harbors of banality.

My footsteps away from childhood into looming adult obligations become silent screams of ambiguity. I tremble over one recurring nightmare that lurks beneath everything else: my body tangled with jungle vines; my tongue blackened by involuntary death; outrage spilling over my lips like drops of blood and sputum; and righteous indignation dripping down my chin onto a sweltering heart. Vietnam. God-damned Vietnam. That public nightmare casts shadows across all western nations, narrowing just to me and my future.

I escape on sandbars surrounding seasons passing slowly and see starlight reflect in laggard muddy waters. I drink warm beer, lay on my back in sunburned sand, and watch the Big Dipper pour cold loneliness through me. I float down a forever river, concerning myself with connectivity and relevance and legacy.

I attempt first love. Brilliant ripples of ardor radiate around me in moments when I race in circles with those first discoveries of growing up. I recruit accomplices and kiss young women to learn about the ephemeral addiction of touch. I discover the power of eroticism. And in the twilight of my morning mind, I live many stories filled with romance, sometimes shuttered with anguish over abruptly love lost.

Trust falls from grace and slaps my face with Rule Number One: *There are no safe romantic harbors; all relationships entail risks of vulnerability, trust, and betrayal.*

Music wanders from eight-track stereos across blowing winds of uncertainty, filling me with doubt, exhilaration, bombast, and gall. Guitars are twangy and sweet and swift. Drums punctuate my youthful, lofty ideals. The beat—beats me, beats me, beats me. I listen to protest songs from Bob Dylan, Joan Baez, and Barry McGuire and shroud myself in bell-bottom trousers like every other budding iconoclast.

Great rock 'n' roll delivers a momentous public dream: a poignant fantasy to have been one of the melodic messengers of youth, to sing the lyrics that are the mood of a generation—inspiring me to absorb and communicate the ideals of a counterculture: Woodstock Nation, the myth of a New America rising from a military-industrial complex of domination, separation, exclusion, and fear.

I listen to every song, born from either crystal or needle and hear the ballads of hopefulness along with the angry antiwar songs. Precise harmonies carry me to audiences who love my message, scream for me. Concert halls full of insatiable fans admire my honesty and humanity, my brief, clear visions of a different style of living, a different set of human priorities

And I clear my callow eyes to understand Rule Number Two: *Within a single song lyric can be found the instructions one needs for how to live with nobility and honesty.*

Friends I find along the way are appreciated. They wake up with me. Boys become men as we hold our cups into the wellspring to find visions and possibilities of this time, together. We sit in stuffy coffee houses, eat peanuts from the shell, litter the floors, and laugh about puberty. Then with fake I.D.'s, we burrow into musty bars reeking with stale beer and steal private moments between gregarious chugs. We smoke Marlboros, drink pitchers of 3.2 beer, and hold on to a televised fantasy of how life should be. We sometimes drive fast in unimpressive cars with ashtrays full of fading fairytales.

Our arguments last late into the night. No one is completely right, but neither is anyone entirely wrong. We warm to a struggle of growing up in a time of social and political revolution. Our insights make the journey authentic and true. I learn the importance of a slogan inciting French social and political protests, a modern-day epitaph for a broken society: "It is forbidden to forbid." All prohibitions are hereby prohibited.

Then Rule Number Three tiptoes into consciousness as my groggy head clears: *Expand yourself: the path to truth requires communication with many differing views of mortal existence.*

My awakening takes me somewhere beyond the senses. I wake to a demanding dilettante and meet a determined wanderer. Yes, the duty animal slithers into my mind and bites me where it hurts. But the poet also blooms during soft moments of transcendent appreciation.

Everything is deconstructed. The old strictures become irrelevant; mangy, arcane philosophies grow tiresome. Some days I think I have the right value system because I wear Dingo boots and Levi's jeans. In another thought, I gain primal wisdom about change that will nurture me through future years of rigorous maturity. Wait long enough, and change happens. The storyline of struggle recycles.

My eyes blink alert; I stretch wistfully, charge forward defiantly, and I unfold my mind to the psychodramas of a new era, lit by the lusty, bright, spiritual, strobing, paisley, unsettling, psychedelic black light of 1969.

CHAPTER SEVENTEEN

Afterword: Woodstock— Toward A Better America?

By Brent Green

Woodstock has been described as a watershed: seminal, formative, and game-changing. Pundits who have attempted to contain the Baby Boomer generation in a tidy sociological package have sometimes pointed at Woodstock in summary, occasionally with derision for the hedonistic overtones this mud-splattered event can represent in mainstream memory.

Woodstock means little of enduring consequence until we place it in the larger context of a society unraveling around the newest generation of young adults, a dominant and dominating cohort of questioners and protesters.

From their parents' generation, the "Greatest Generation," they had absorbed rich idealism for time-honored principles of social and economic justice. These lessons came to them through school civics classes and from moral teachings inculcated by nonprofit organizations such as 4-H, Boy Scouts, and Girl Scouts. Through these moral torchbearers, young Americans learned the fundamentals of democracy and nuanced meaning of "we the people" *and* "a more perfect union." From the world they were inheriting, however, they had discovered discontinuities and hypocrisies.

The first generation to grow up with broadcast television had learned in childhood to stare down orthodoxy and propaganda as if a gunslinging Marshal Matt Dillon, the tall and virtuous lead character in *Gunsmoke*, a wildly popular television series of twenty years duration. The same could be written of other western archetypical heroes instilling subtle moral lessons such as Clayton Moore and Jay Silverheels, lead actors in *The Lone Ranger*, or the righteous and hardworking Cartwright men of the TV-series *Bonanza*. This generation learned early in life to recognize and challenge disturbing gaps between moral principles and institutional and governmental actions.

Woodstock was just one major event with national impact that blasted through 1969, creating context while revealing collective motivations. The final year of the tumultuous sixties included discordant Richard Milhous Nixon succeeding Lyndon Baines Johnson as the 37th president of the United States. U.S. troops stationed in Vietnam crested at 549,500.

Three hundred students stormed and occupied Harvard University's administration building in a spellbinding demonstration of street theater. Charles Manson's LSD-crazed cult members executed actress Sharon Tate and four others, including Tate's unborn child. This was all before the turbulent autumn featuring the largest peaceful protest of war in U.S. history on October 15th, the Moratorium Against the War in Vietnam. And that's not even close to half of the events impinging on the worldview of millions of young people coming of age all at once.

Woodstock was not merely a late summer concert showcasing some of the best rock 'n' roll bands of the sixties. It was an interlude arriving in the context of more social and political upheaval than most Americans had ever witnessed, especially the nation's youth. It was a disorganized but peaceful prelude to a forthcoming breakdown between government and governed when citizen determination would finally end an unpopular and deadly war—but not before the horrific cost of 58,220 American lives.

To become embroiled in the counterculture and idealism this festival represented did not require actual attendance among the estimated 400,000 who successfully made the trek to Bethel, New York, and Max Yasgur's dairy farm. Political upheaval, disintegrating racial relations, burgeoning feminism, environmental degradation, and rock 'n' roll culture enveloped a generation, inundating the youth cohort from all corners of the nation while forging shared attitudes of anti-authoritarianism and consciousness-expansion.

From Alaska to Florida to New York, young people crisscrossed the country for peace and love in a time of rage and resentment. Most wanted to do the right thing, and to them this meant standing strong against received authority and the hegemony of paternalistic elites steering the nation through a wasteful Vietnam War, not to mention decades of institutional repression of minorities and women. Woodstock at once represented the improbable and the possible: just three spins of the globe, three short days—an interruption of business-as-usual. Yet the influences of this brief span of history persist now in the 21st century.

I witnessed remnants of the Woodstock era as protesters clamored along downtown Denver's 16th Street Mall during the Democratic National Convention in 2008, their faces lit up with passions and high purposes. Two months later, I felt a reassuring presence of shared citizenship in Civic Center Park when more than 100,000 gathered peacefully to hear words of hope and renewal from their next president, improbably a man of

African-American descent with a strangely un-American sounding name: Barack Hussein Obama.

I have seen vestiges of Woodstock during recent Women's Marches on Washington, a movement gathering attention to and providing education about women's issues but also a plethora of other social movements. The stated goal of the Women's March is to provide a bulwark against "the rising tide of authoritarianism, misogyny, white nationalism, racism, anti-Semitism, homophobia, transphobia, xenophobia, Islamophobia, ableism, classism, and ageism." Many of the same phobias and isms troubled young Boomers fifty years ago and fomented rebellion at all levels of society and culture. The inaugural 2017 March involved over 4 million protesters in the United States, perhaps the largest single-day protest in U.S. history.

I have seen Woodstock-era passions rise again during the March For Our Lives demonstrations in 2018, the vociferous and emotional protests in support of stronger gun violence prevention measures. Organized and directed by students from Marjory Stoneman Douglas High School in Parkland, Fla., these young people—many of whom are grandchildren of Baby Boomers—quickly emerged as national anti-gun leaders in the wake of the shooting that left 17 of their classmates assassinated on Valentine's Day, 2018.

Finally, on a softer and more melodic note, I am reminded of Woodstock's "Three Days of Peace and Music" through today's diverse music and arts festivals such as Burning Man, Coachella, Bonnaroo, South by Southwest (SXSW), and Lollapalooza.

The 50th anniversary of Woodstock could be meaningless if nothing meaningful has survived other than a passing historical footnote. But when we peer beyond throngs of young Boomers wearing tie-dyed t-shirts, battered denim bellbottoms, and eccentric tribal costumes while considering the present "state of the union," we see an extraordinarily similar America five decades later: arguably, a nation still striving to achieve its loftiest humanistic values and ideals. With suppressive forces lurking behind our nation's best intentions, the quest to achieve social and economic justice carries on apace, renewed by the fire and ferment of youthful passions, coupled with the earned wisdom of aging Baby Boomers who have been transported from Woodstock across five decades, their dreams and designs for a better nation still persistent.

About the Authors

Several years ago, Brent Green imagined a retrospective tribute to the final year of the 1960s, to be published during the year's 50th anniversary. At first, he envisioned a solo journey of personal revelations and writing. Realizing that a book about such a complex historical period would benefit from more than a single voice, he reached out to seven colleagues and friends to see if they might join him in writing remembrances and revelations about 1969, one of the most remarkable years of the 20th century. The only dictum asked of these writers was for them to be emotionally truthful about the final year of the 1960s, whether through nonfiction, creative nonfiction or fictional stories.

Brent has always felt fortunate to know talented writers and communicators—people who have accomplished many noteworthy achievements during fruitful careers. His collaborators agreed to participate with shared enthusiasm. They wrote independently without reading each other's contributions until the project was nearly finished. This assured a collection of unique perspectives. The following biographies are more than descriptions of personal and professional achievements. They also serve to chronicle representatives of a passionate generation reaching its full potential throughout adulthood, as social and political change agents and business thought leaders.

Carol Orsborn, Ph.D.

Carol Orsborn is founder/editor of *Fierce with Age, the Digest of Boomer Wisdom, Inspiration and Spirituality*. She has written 30 books for and about the Boomer generation, including *The Spirituality of Age: A Seeker's Guide to Growing Older*, winner of gold, category of *Consciously Aging*, Nautilus Book Awards (with Robert L. Weber, Ph.D.) and her most recent book, *Angelica's Last Breath*, a novel inspired by Tolstoy's *The Death of Ivan Ilyich*.

Carol has been a voice for the Boomer generation since the 1960s, while a student leader at the University of California, Berkeley. At the time, her commentary on the spirit of the women in her generational cohort captured the attention of national media including *Mademoiselle Magazine* and *The New York Times* and won her positions as a columnist at both *The Chicago Daily News* and *San Francisco Chronicle*. She has continued to inspire as well as to articulate insights about her generation through every life stage they've transited together over the past five decades, with appearances on *The Today Show*, *Oprah*, *NBC Nightly News* and many more. She has also been invited to speak for a wide range of industries and associations in the U.S. and Europe which include individuals 50+ in their target demographic. Clients have included Ford, Prudential, AARP and many others.

Carol graduated Phi Beta Kappa from the University of California, Berkeley in 1970 with a Bachelor of Arts degree in Communications. While there, she served in various capacities on the student newspaper *The Daily Californian*, including Arts Editor and columnist. After a distinguished career founding and running one of the country's leading independent public relations agencies culminating with her work for Fleishman Hillard, she took a second career sabbatical and received her Master of Theology and then a Doctorate in the History and Critical Theory of Religion from Vanderbilt University, specializing in adult and spiritual development. She currently serves on the Board of Visitors for Vanderbilt Divinity School. She has taught at Pepperdine, Loyola Marymount, and Georgetown Universities and has presented at the Omega Institute, the American Society of Aging, Sage-ing International and many more. Carol leads the *Conscious Aging Book Club* for Parnassus Books. Her blog *Older, Wiser, Fiercer*, which is also the subject of her next book, is available at CarolOrsborn.com.

She lives on the Cumberland River in Madison, Tennessee with her husband Dan, who is lead guitar and vocalist in the classic sixties rock band *What?!* She is the mother of two adult children and has two grandsons and three dogs.

David Cogswell

Born smack dab in the middle of America, in Topeka, Kansas, three months before the midpoint of the 20th Century, David Cogswell came of age just as the fiery social conflicts of the '60s were coming to a rolling boil. His consciousness was formed in the cauldron of the anti-Vietnam War movement, and as the twig was bent, so grew the tree.

David left Kansas in the early '70s to work in a traveling nightclub band and settled in the late '70s in New York City. There he continued to work as a musician, ran a book and music kiosk at Fifth Avenue at Central Park, and opened a bookstore in Hoboken, New Jersey.

During these various adventures, he kept up a disciplined practice of writing, and once he was settled, the practice developed into a career as a freelance writer dealing with social issues, arts and entertainment, politics, culture and travel.

Since that time, he has published thousands of articles in publications that include the *Chicago Tribune*, the *Los Angeles Times*, *Fortune*, Fox News.com, *Luxury Travel* magazine, *Travel Weekly*, *Travel Market Report*, and TravelPulse.com.

As a travel writer, he has been able to travel frequently and widely to all seven continents, developing a global perspective through firsthand experience of a vast range of cultural and geographical differences experienced in many African countries, Antarctica, Brazil, China, Russia, Italy, Greece, France, Spain,

Germany, the U.K., Alaska, Peru, the Galapagos, Cuba, Vietnam, Cambodia, India, and others.

He is the author of four books in the *For Beginners* series, on Noam Chomsky, Howard Zinn, Existentialism and Unions, and has contributed to several other books, including *Fortunate Son, The Making of an American President,* by J.H. Hatfield; *Ambushed: The Hidden History of the Bush Family* by Toby Rogers; and *America's Autopsy Report,* by John Kaminski.

Richard Adler

Richard Adler was born in New York, grew up in Colorado, went to college in Massachusetts, and came to Berkeley in 1964 to go to graduate school, where he still was in 1969. He then went to Ohio for two years to teach at Oberlin College, then came back to California where he arrived just in time to experience the emergence of Silicon Valley.

Today, Richard is a Distinguished Fellow at Institute for the Future (IFTF), Palo Alto, CA. He is also principal of People & Technology, a research and consulting firm based in Silicon Valley.

At IFTF, he directed a multi-client research program entitled *Baby Boomers: The Next 20 Years*. He also conducted a project on "global networks of innovation in aging" and led a major project on the future of caregiving funded by the Robert Wood Johnson Foundation.

In 2017, he led the effort to get his home community of Cupertino designated as an "age-friendly city" by the World Health Organization. He is currently a member of the Advisory Board for the Santa Clara County Area Agency on Aging.

From 1990 to 1996, Richard was vice-president for development at SeniorNet, a national nonprofit whose mission is to introduce older adults to computers and the Internet. Richard wrote the organization's first business plan, conducted the first-ever survey of computer use by older adults, and helped to build a national network of more than 200 SeniorNet Learning Centers.

Richard has spoken and written extensively on aging, healthcare, and technology. His publications include *Age Wave, Meet Tech Wave: Closing the Digital Divide* (*CSA Journal*, 2017); *Catalyzing Technology to Support Family Caregivers* (NAC, 2014); and *The Great Retirement Divide* (in *Longevity Rules*, Eskaton, 2011). He served as guest editor for the Fall 2010 issue of *Generations*, the journal of the American Society on Aging, on "the future of aging."

Richard has also had a long association with the Aspen Institute, for which he has written reports on topics ranging from institutional innovation to telecommunications policy. Examples include *The Exponential Shift* (2017); *Making the Invisible Visible* (2016); *Preparing for a 5G World* (2016); *Navigating Continual Disruption* (2015); and *Updating Rules of the Digital Road (2012)*. His non-Aspen tech-related writings include *Toward a Better Understanding of Internet Economics* (Columbia University, 2018); *After Broadband: Imagining Hyperconnected Futures* (Wharton, 2012); and *The Future of Broadband* (Broadband for America, 2012*)*.

Richard has taught at Stanford and UCLA and was a Research Fellow at the Harvard Graduate School of Education. He holds a BA from Harvard, an MA from the University of California at Berkeley, and an MBA from the McLaren School of Business at the University of San Francisco.

Bob Moses

Bob Moses graduated from Hamilton College in Clinton, NY, in 1968.* To delay either a definitive career choice or possible marching orders, he applied to join VISTA (Volunteers in Service to America), the U.S. domestic Peace Corps program initiated by LBJ in 1965. Accepted, he departed on an 8,000-mile motorcycle trip throughout the U.S., awaiting assignment, which arrived in early 1969 to New Orleans.

There he started a community newspaper with the goal of uniting disparate black neighborhoods to address common social and political concerns. The newspaper quickly became controversial when it started monitoring police visitations to black neighborhoods and reporting on alleged incidents of police brutality.

After completing his VISTA service in 1971, he attended the University of Denver Law School. He dropped out after two years to start, in Colorado, the first newspaper in the U.S. targeted to older people. He published the paper for the next 18 years. During that time, he wrote a regular column, *Old Man Moses*, focused on ageism, the rights of older people, and the challenges of growing older. He was an early board member of the Gray Panthers, founded by Maggie Kuhn, and published the original *Gray Panther* newspaper.

Over his long career of advocacy for older people, he received numerous local and national awards and recognition, including the 1987 Public Service Award from the American College of Health Care Administrators.

Following the sale of his newspaper in 1988, Bob started a nationwide marketing company targeting older consumers, from which he retired in 2017. He continues to work as a marketing consultant and freelance writer. A selection of his writings may be found at bobwrytes.com.

Bob Moses (Hamilton '68) should not be confused with fellow Hamilton College graduate and civil rights leader Robert Parris Moses ('56), who founded the Student Non-Violent Coordinating Committee (SNCC) in 1960 and co-founded the Mississippi Freedom Democratic Party in 1963.

Jed Diamond, Ph.D.

Jed Diamond has been helping men and their families for fifty years. He is the founder/director of MenAlive and is a leader in the field of gender medicine and men's health. He is the author of fifteen books including international best-sellers *Male Menopause, Surviving Male Menopause: A Guide for Women and Men, The Irritable Male Syndrome: Understanding and Managing the 4 Key Causes of Depression and Aggression,* and *Looking for Love in All the Wrong Places*. His forthcoming book, *14 Rules for Becoming Your Own Man: Your Guide for Living Fully, Loving Deeply, and Making a Difference in the World*, will be published in 2019.

The year 1969 was a turning point in his personal and professional life. He had been deeply involved with student protests against the Vietnam War at U.C. Berkeley between 1965 and 1968. When his son, Jemal, was born on November 21, 1969, he made a vow that he would be a different kind of father than his father was able to be for him and to help change the world so that men could escape from the "Man Box," a set of outmoded rules and restrictions that harm both men and women.

Jed has been in a men's group that has been meeting for forty years. He is a featured writer for *The Good Men Project*, where 3.5 million people read his weekly articles, including: "The One Thing Men Want More Than Sex," "The 5 Stages of Love and

Why Too Many Stop at Stage 3," and "7 Things That Make a Man Feel Loved."

His work has been featured in major newspapers throughout the United States including the *New York Times*, *Boston Globe*, *Wall Street Journal*, and *The Los Angeles Times*. He has been featured on more than 1,000 radio and TV programs including The View with Barbara Walters, *Good Morning America*, *Today Show*, *CNN-360 with Anderson Cooper*, CBS, NBC, Fox News, and *To Tell the Truth*. He produced and created a nationally televised special on Male Menopause for PBS-TV.

Jed's Ph.D. is in International Health and his dissertation, *Male vs. Female Depression: Why Men Act Out and Women Act In*, offers a new understanding of healing depression in men. Visit him at www.MenAlive.com to get a free eBook and chapter from his recent memoir, *My Distant Dad: Healing the Family Father Wound*.

Greg Dobbs

Greg Dobbs started his professional career as a journalist in 1969 when he was hired as the editor to then-radio icon Paul Harvey.

But growing up, Greg didn't intend to be a journalist. He intended to be a lawyer. However, while at the University of California at Berkeley, Greg got caught up in demonstrations known as the Free Speech Movement. He wasn't caught up as a participant, just as a spectator. But a fascinated spectator, who  began to realize that reporters were getting paid to be where he was for nothing. So, one day, Greg screwed up the courage to go up to one reporter and ask if the guy always got to go where the action was. The reporter said "Sure, kid," and Greg was hooked.

Since then, Greg says there have been a few days when he cursed that reporter for pointing him toward his career, but when he looks at the bigger picture, he won't trade it for anything. Because over almost five decades for two television networks, including roughly two decades as a foreign and war correspondent, Greg got to go wherever the action was. He reported on history-making stories from more than 80 countries—from South Africa to Afghanistan, from Iran to Egypt, from Saudi Arabia to the Soviet Union, Vietnam to Venezuela, Libya to Liberia, Panama to Poland. He also reported from 49 states; he has never set foot in Rhode Island and at this point in life, probably never will.

Greg's career has had its dark side—he covered eight wars and many massive natural disasters—but he also got to report live from the Kennedy Space Center for 35 Space Shuttle launches, and Charles and Diana's (ill-fated) Royal Wedding, and he got to cover six presidential campaigns and fly on Air Force One.

Along the way, Greg has been honored with three Emmy Awards and the "Distinguished Service Award" from the Society of Professional Journalists, plus a perch in the Denver Press Club Hall of Fame.

Greg also hosted an award-winning program for six years for Rocky Mountain PBS and wrote weekly op-ed columns for *The Rocky Mountain News*, then for *The Denver Post*. He has written two books (*"Life in the Wrong Lane"* is about a foreign correspondent's wacky life).

Greg and his wife Carol have been married for 45 years. He has three grown children and two grandkids.

Robert William Case

Several decades ago, Robert William Case lived the life of a conservative, introverted lawyer in Littleton, Colorado. His kids were still in high school, about to graduate. Then, the Columbine High School massacre happened. Like a heavy rock falling into the placid waters of their community, the waves spread out in all directions, modulated into ripples, and impacted everything in their path.

For a long time afterward, Robert tried to follow familiar habits and routines. Kept his head down. Kept moving. But discontent was creeping in. Fissures appeared in the walls of his automatic deposit, paycheck-driven world. He was sharing it with a mischievous alter ego: one that enjoyed awakening in the early morning hours to journal for a while before heading off to work. Little by little a story emerged, a short work of fiction titled *Daedalus Rising*, inspired by the archetypal inventor and father from Greek mythology, the man who invented the first pair of working wings. The book was published in 2008.

His days of practicing law were numbered. Robert was finding his own voice, written and spoken. He discovered that he enjoyed being on stage, telling stories, and hearing others laugh and applaud. Today he can testify that just being a bystander witness to a mass casualty event like Columbine alters the course of a lifetime.

Robert's first acting role was in a three-act show performed at the 2005 Boulder Fringe Festival. He went on to play Ralph Waldo Emerson in *Walden-The Ballad of Thoreau* and Morrie Schwartz in *Tuesdays with Morrie* at the Festival Playhouse in Arvada, Colorado. In 2011, he was a cast member of an improv show at the Bovine Theater in Denver titled *Susan and Her Magic Eight Ball.*

His second book is an elegant adventure novel, published in 2014, that reimagines the Greek myth of the boy with wings who flew too close to the sun. Drawing on this wellspring of ancient wisdom, *Icarus and the Wing Builder,* tells an epic tale of love and betrayal and coming of age on the Minoan sailing ships of the Aegean Sea. It raises the question: Did anyone but his father see Icarus fall from the sky? The book provides an alternative history, telling the story of what really happened in the sky that day.

Robert's latest publication is an essay about his own coming of age in the American heartland during 1969, the highwater year of the undeclared and escalating war in Vietnam. In *Are You Still Listening? 1969 Stories & Essays,* Robert joins with an eclectic group of eight eminent authors to commemorate that tumultuous year. Many of the political and social issues that swept across the nation in that era have cycled back around in this fiftieth anniversary year. Hopefully, this time we can collectively do a better job of resolving them.

In his spare time, Robert is an advocate for health, vitality, and renewable energy. He recently completed a journey across the continental USA by touring bicycle in two stages, completing the western half during the summer of 2017 and the eastern half during the summer of 2018. More information about bicycle adventure and living well at any age can be found at: www.BicyclePoet.com. His poetry has appeared in *The Colorado Lawyer.*

Brent Green

Brent Green has been a community leader and nonprofit organizer throughout his academic and professional careers spanning over four decades.

During college in the late sixties at the University of Kansas, he chaired an influential Student Advisory Committee. This outspoken council persuaded administrators to eliminate dorm closing hours, create the first coeducational dorm, and discontinue sending students' grade reports home to parents as required, a formative leadership experience.

Brent began his goal to explore the realities and implications of the 1960s through a literary novel, *Noble Chaos*, the first historical novel capturing the turbulent Vietnam War era within the revolutionary setting of a Midwestern university. An early version of the manuscript received literary recognition from authors and editors in the annual *Colorado Gold* fiction writing competition, sponsored by Rocky Mountain Fiction Writers.

He has served on many community boards and organizing committees, including the World Cycling Championships, Junior Achievement's *National Business Leadership Hall of Fame Conference*, as Vice President for programs of the Business Marketing Association and the Rocky Mountain Direct Marketing Association, and as a board member for ten years and chairman of the Colorado Springs Convention & Visitors Bureau.

Brent has received national awards for two essays and a magazine feature article from *Writer's Digest* through the magazine's annual writing competitions. *Marketing to Leading-Edge Baby Boomers* and *Generation Reinvention*, his business books, provide thought-leading examinations of the sociology and psychology of the Boomer generation. His *Boomers* blog is an online journal about Baby Boomers, and the influence of this generation is having on business and aging. He has been a contributor to the *Huffington Post* and written for CNBC as part of the ramp up to a Tom Brokaw television documentary on the Boomer generation. Following the passing of his sister, he wrote *Questions of the Spirit: The Quest for Understanding at A Time of Loss*, an inspired nonfiction book about grief, bereavement, and loss. He has also written *WARRIOR: The Life and Lessons of a Man Who Beat Cancer for 57 Years*, a fictional story inspired by Mark Crooks, Ph.D., a pioneer in the field of wellness.

As a creative director and copywriter, Brent has received over fifty awards for creative excellence, including the Direct Marketing Association's International Gold Echo Award, the highest worldwide distinction in direct marketing.

www.ingramcontent.com/pod-product-compliance
Lightning Source LLC
Chambersburg PA
CBHW021948290426
44108CB00012B/993